Follow The Money

—m—

How To Achieve Prosperity By Doing The Things The Rich Do

Thomas K Lamb

Copyright © 2014 Thomas K Lamb
All rights reserved.

ISBN: 1495392651
ISBN 13: 9781495392658
Library of Congress Control Number: 2014902461
CreateSpace Independent Publishing Platform
North Charleston, South Carolina

Acknowledgments

To Al who made me go to that fateful 401(k) meeting. To the late great Johnny Hock who knew so much about investing that he could make sitting in traffic on the George Washington Bridge or Washington Beltway fascinating. To Jimmy who, although he didn't always invest the difference wisely, sure knew how to live below his means. To Shavonna, Nick, Buda, Andrew, and Dylan who not only gave me faith in this project, but give me faith in the future. To Mom who thinks Shakespeare doesn't hold a candle to me as a writer. And to Trish, my partner in countless adventures, my wife, and most importantly, my best friend

Table of Contents

Acknowledgments	iii
Table of Contents	v
Foreword	vii
Introduction	xi
Chapter One: Taking Stock	1
Chapter Two: Start!	7
Chapter Three: What These Things Are	13
Chapter Four: The Best Path To Financial Independence For The Working Person	33
Chapter Five: The Emergency Fund	45
Chapter Six: Credit: A Double-Edged Sword	53
Chapter Seven: A House: To Buy or Not to Buy, That is the Question	61
Chapter Eight: Taxable Investing: The Arena of Joy and Pain	73
Chapter Nine: Keep What You've Got	87
Chapter Ten: Charlatans and Rip-off Artists	101
Chapter Eleven: Giving It All Away (OK, Just Some of It)	107
Chapter Twelve: You: The Best Investment You Can Make	113
Conclusion	125
Resources	127

Foreword

The rich seemingly have all the advantages in this day and age. After-tax income rose 201% for the top one percent between 1979 and 2010, but only 40% for the 60% of Americans who make up the (rapidly shrinking) middle class. The top income tax rate was 70% in 1979; in 2014 the top marginal tax rate paid by the very highest earners is 39.6% The richest one percent of Americans owned 35% of all the wealth in America in 2007, while the bottom 90% owned just 27%. Many rich people get into elite universities simply because one or both parents went there. Legacy trumps merit any day of the week at these places. Poor people get welfare; when rich business owners get handouts from the government they're called "subsidies." Though the more egregious subsidies go to highly profitable agribusinesses and oil and gas companies, there are other subsidies companies get on the sly. When workers at big box stores and fast food chains qualify for public assistance because they are paid less than poverty wages, that's a subsidy we the taxpayers provide to a business whether or not we patronize that business. The restaurant business is possibly the biggest welfare queen of all. There is no other business that has been able to cut a deal with the government whereby minimum wage laws don't apply to them at all. Restaurants are the only businesses in America where owners are allowed to let their customers pay their employees (or not) directly. In 1965 the typical CEO made 20 times more than the lowest paid worker. In 2013 that figure was 354 times. It's good to be rich in a country where corporations are people and Congress is always on sale.

Is any of this fair? Of course not. Life isn't fair. Good looks often eclipse education and experience when hiring decisions are made. No kidding. Can anything be done about it? Not on the macro level. Not as long as we keep electing the same people who, by the very definition of insanity, keep trying the same things that haven't worked in the past while expecting a different result the next time around. Not as long as the conventional wisdom holds that, not only are people who don't have jobs bums, but people without *good enough* jobs are bums as well. Not as long as relentless cost-cutting becomes the *raison d'etre* of American business. In an economy that is 70% consumer-driven, things will only continue to get worse as real wages continue to fall behind inflation. With few visionary CEOs (such as Costco's Craig Jelinek who cries all the way to the bank by treating his employees well or a Henry Ford who discovered he could make a lot of money selling cars to his own employees if he paid them enough to afford them), the quality of American life will continue to erode as it has done for more than 30 years now.

Can anything be done on the micro level, that is, in a single individual's life? Yes. Though I despise the tired old cliché "pull yourself up by the bootstraps" (as if laziness and not four applicants for each available job is the reason unemployment exists), the average working person is not completely at the mercy of events. Good or bad decisions made now can have a profound impact on the outcome of your life.

There are, in fact, everyday people who start out middle- or working class who manage to join the ranks of the rich. It's certainly not easy to do, but it is done nevertheless. Although many of the superrich enjoy arguably unfair advantages from the very beginning (aside from many of them being buffoons with gaudy jewelry, impractical cars, and debutante balls in the year 2014), there is a whole strata of rich people who have gotten that way on pure (more or less) merit. Most of these people are hidden in plain sight. They might be your neighbors, coworkers, or the guy in the next aisle sprucing-up his wardrobe at Walmart. Unlike the superrich (or those who merely want people to believe they're rich) who like to advertise their money, these people get and stay rich beneath the radar. Wealth is largely a function of what we do and don't do. There is a reason rich families often stay rich and poor families remain poor generation after generation. What we *do* is far more an important factor than, hereditary rich people notwithstanding, who we *are*. Rich people simply do things that make (or keep) them rich, and poor people do things that keep them poor. The calculus is just that simple. It's very easy to get poor, but the easiest way to get rich is to follow the money, that is, to cultivate the habits rich people have.

Follow The Money

There are a few basic ways people get wealth. Some people inherit their money or gain it through questionable means (think CEOs who get millions of dollars to go away after they've run a formerly profitable company into the ground). A tiny percentage of the wealthy win their money or are born with gifts (such as the ability to throw a football) that the vast majority of us don't have. Unfortunately, this group has a terrible track record of actually *staying* rich. Even more unfortunately, many parents, under the delusion that their kid is something special, push sports at the expense of academics. Your kid is far more likely to get into Harvard Medical School than the NFL. A very large percentage of millionaires are people who have started and grown small businesses. These people are the embodiment of the American Dream. Unlike the rich who get that way merely because they are lucky enough to have the right connections, these are the people who risk their own money, drag themselves out of bed at three a.m. to meet the police because an alarm has gone off, and often find themselves working many more hours than they worked as an employee. Finally, there are the investors.

Running the gamut from Warren Buffett to the person who has just made his or her first 401(k) contribution, investors are those people who grow wealth mostly by owning businesses. In contrast to entrepreneurs who may own companies with names such as "Pete's Plumbing" or "Hannah's Home Decorating," however, these people own companies with names such as Coca-Cola, Johnson & Johnson, General Electric, and Boeing. If the person in the cube next to yours or out on the factory floor is one of the secretly affluent, chances are almost certain that he or she is an investor.

Investing is the most reliable way to build a prosperous life. It is certainly not without risk, but the risks of investing (as opposed to speculating) are nowhere near those an entrepreneur takes. Where roughly half of all small businesses fail within the first five years, many of the companies investors own have been in business since the 19th Century. Though I have nothing but respect for those entrepreneurs who roll the dice and make their fortunes ethically, this book is geared toward the individual investor. While not everyone who invests will become rich, anyone who ends up better-off than he or she would have otherwise been meets the criteria for success. Many investors who never become rich do, in fact, become at least well-off. Though most of us would love to achieve the title "millionaire," there is definitely something to be said for having several tens or hundreds of thousands extra in the bank at retirement.

Introduction

If investing one's way to affluence is not only possible, but not even particularly hard from the standpoint of knowing what to do, why do so relatively few people do it? We are largely a nation of financial illiterates. Few schools offer, let alone require, courses in even basic personal finance. Financially illiterate parents, as a rule, do not raise financially savvy kids. If there is one glaring difference between rich people and poor people it's that rich people put a premium on education, even that informal education that is passed from parent to child at the dinner table. Rich people, in other words, are much more inclined than poor people to discuss financial matters with their children.

Human nature plays a huge role in the financial success or failure of an individual. Unfortunately, it seems the human brain is hard-wired for failure. Inertia, that human tendency to choose to do nothing when given the choice between doing something or nothing, is a major reason that vast numbers of people stay stuck in seemingly inescapable paycheck to paycheck hell their entire working lives. Most people have the best intentions to sign-up for that 401(k) or to get serious about paying-off the credit cards, but somehow never get around to it. A New Year's resolution becomes a spring cleaning resolution, then a July 4th resolution, then a Labor Day resolution, then yet again a New Year's resolution. Meanwhile the clock is ticking. Years turn into decades and retirement dreams become pipe dreams.

Ironically, many rich people learn to harness their inertia. Some people actually get rich through their own laziness. In the same way it takes initiative to do something, it often takes initiative to stop doing something. Some people sign up for automatic investments and, though they might later convince themselves that they could really use the money being deducted from their paychecks or bank accounts *right now*, never get around to actually stopping those investments. Other people save themselves from terrible financial decisions because they hesitate too long on that "once in a lifetime" deal or are too busy watching television to go shopping at the mall or buy that new car they can ill-afford.

One other problem that can be ascribed to human nature is that we tend to believe what we want to believe, logic oftentimes notwithstanding. Crooks have been cashing in on this foible for millennia. We have all seen those Saturday afternoon infomercials where some guy pitches his can't fail stock trading or real estate for just pennies on the dollar "system." We convince ourselves (or maybe just entertain the idea) that perhaps this guy really does know the "secrets" of wealth. Unfortunately (for his customers anyway), his "secret" is that he sells books, tapes, and seminars full of useless mumbo-jumbo for $29.95 a pop. It's highly unlikely that a municipality would sell a property worth hundreds of thousands for just a few hundred bucks in back taxes. It is utterly and completely impossible to consistently time the stock market. If it could be done, someone would have done it already. This person's name would be known to every household. Nowhere is this vagary of human nature more harmful (and the charlatans more evil) than in cases where "natural cures" for terrible diseases are being peddled. If a diet could cure cancer, it would be common knowledge. Period.

Another trait seemingly built into human nature is that we often both over- and underestimate ourselves. We tell ourselves that we could never learn that investing stuff because we're just not smart enough. Those charts and tickers in the business section of the newspaper are a foreign language to us. The truth is that we are smart enough, but are just never taught. One way in which we overestimate ourselves is to say "I don't need to save for retirement because I'll be working until I drop dead." Tragically, this is often a decision we don't get to make. We are three times more likely to become disabled than to die. There comes a point for many of us where we are simply unable to work anymore.

The absolute worst particularity of human nature, one that is mandatory to overcome in order to build an affluent life, is that we are herd animals. We chase phantoms *en masse* and run off the cliff together. If there is one trait that sets the financially successful person apart from everyone else it is that he or she has learned to run against the herd.

Warren Buffet's personal mantra is "be greedy when others are fearful; be fearful when others are greedy." This pretty much sums-up the "secret" of wealth. It is, alas, much easier said than done to actually put this into practice. For those able to do it, however, the rewards can be immense.

As the 1900s gave way to the 2000s, there was a bubble in technology stocks. Anyone buying technology stocks at the time just couldn't seem to go wrong. Companies that traded for 150 times earnings (fifteen times is generally considered a fair value) kept going up in price. Companies that didn't actually make any money went up as well. One icon of the times was a sock puppet that advertised products for just such a company. This puppet would later become emblematic of the euphoria and ensuing hangover when the party finally ended. Ane end it did. In March of 2000 the bubble burst. The same people who had overestimated their investing prowess found that some of their investments had gone all the way to zero. The herd rushed out of the now collapsed stock market bubble and immediately started inflating a new investment bubble.

The real estate bubble was to culminate seven years later in the Great Recession. Though the recession technically ended in 2009, we are still feeling the effects of it to this day. Except for a few cautionary voices, only a seeming idiot would have bet against real estate in the mid-2000s. Money was cheap and flowed freely. House prices were *doubling* each year in places like Las Vegas and Florida. Real estate was such an apparent no-brainer that there were new TV shows devoted entirely to house flipping. When the whole house of cards collapsed at the end of 2007, it wasn't just real estate that went down hard. Stocks got killed and jobs were lost. Whole industries had to be saved by the government. The herd, yet again, changed course. This time recklessness was replaced with paralyzing fear. Legions of regular people quit contributing to their 401(k) s. Already burned in their real estate and stock investments, the herd thought it could cut its losses. It was, by this time, already way too late for that. Those who stopped contributing, or worse, cashed out their stock investments (thus locking-in their losses) would live to regret it. Deeply.

The stock market reached its nadir in March of 2009. Though the average 401(k) investor was now numb from the relentless beating he or she had taken, those people with the mindset that plans for (and usually results in) future prosperity began to salivate. The fire sale was on. Warren Buffett famously said at about this time: "When it's raining gold get a bucket not a thimble." By March 2010 those who had stayed the course by at least not cashing out the stock investments in their 401(k)s were made whole. Those who had gone against the herd and actually continued buying stocks throughout the carnage made money. Those who held on through 2013 made *a lot* of money.

An old cliché says "the rich are just different from you and me." Like so many clichés, there is a strong element of truth in this. The rich certainly aren't better than anyone else. The vast majority are not even particularly smarter. It's an ongoing joke in the financial world that the most successful investors are "B" students and that the "A" students end up working for them. What makes rich people different is that they are able to master their emotions, they do the things that lead to prosperity and avoid doing the things that have the opposite effect, and, most importantly, they execute.

Execution is everything. Getting started, more than any single factor, is the primary determinant of whether we eventually prosper or struggle for a lifetime. Inertia is the reason that time slips through our fingers; tragically, most of us realize this only when it is too late. Time is, if anything, far more critical to building wealth than how much money we make. This is why there are warehouse workers, truck drivers, cosmetologists, and janitors out there with fortunes. The reason for this is compounding.

Compounding is that process where the interest (or earnings) on your money in turn make more money. A thousand dollars at six percent will be $1,060 in a year. If nothing is added it will be $1,123.60 in two years, $1,338.23 in five, and $1,790.84 in ten years. If, on the other hand, money is consistently added paycheck after paycheck (such as in a 401(k)), even in small increments, the snowball effect will be intensified. A thousand dollars becomes two, then ten, then fifty, then a hundred thousand dollars over years and decades. This is how self-made investors achieve wealth. It's not quick, though you already knew there is no reliable way to get rich quick. Though simple, it's not easy. It takes consistency, the ability to keep going, and sometimes nerves of steel as evidenced by those people with the fortitude to stay the course in 2008. It's important to remember, however, that it is possible. The fact that you may come home with dirt under you fingernails each night is immaterial. It's not about *how* you make your money, but what you *do* with your money. The caricature of rich people sitting around a country club scoffing at the "little people" as servants bring them martinis is far more Hollywood than reality. The rich are not an entirely closed class, some sort of American nobility. Somewhere along the line even the most snobbish rich people had an ancestor who, unlike the majority of his peers, executed.

Another trait rich people have is that they are not afraid to pay for expertise. From lawyers, to accountants, to financial advisors, they see money spent to preserve and grow their fortunes as an investment. Happily, paying experts is not necessary for the small investor just starting out. One goal of this book is to give you the financial education you need to lay the foundations of your future prosperity. Most 401(k) plans come with access to financial advice, usually for free.

The old saw that the key to wealth is to live below your means and invest the difference is not too far off the mark. One critical difference between rich people and those who live paycheck to paycheck is in the way they spend.

We have all seen the ostentatious rich on TV with multi-million dollar beach houses in The Hamptons, yachts, $500,000 cars, and private jets. This is not the way most wealthy people live, particularly those wealthy people you rub elbows with regularly whether you realize it or not. Unlike most middle class, working class, and poor people, rich people consider whether the thing they are considering buying is an appreciating or depreciating asset. Appreciating assets are things that become more valuable with age; depreciating assets are things like cars, phones, clothes, and other things whose ultimate destiny is the scrap heap. One of the huge downsides of living in a consumer society is that we are judged by the quality of our stuff. Unfortunately, most of the stuff we buy in an effort to keep up with the Joneses are depreciating assets. When I was in high school any kid whose parents were unable or unwilling to buy their clothes at expensive and trendy mall stores practically assured their kid would never be amongst the high school aristocracy. Ironically, all those expensive clothes are now rotting away in a landfill somewhere. I was one of those kids whose parents would not pay for a label. I see their point now, but sure wish they had bought me stock in Apple with the difference!

Thomas K Lamb

Where many people buy cars they can't really afford, houses that are really just vacuum cleaners of money, and the latest electronic gadgets all in an effort to win the approval of other people (most of whom couldn't care less), rich people buy things such as stocks, bonds, and education. Though the superrich are no more immune to peer pressure than middle- or working class people, there is a group between the mega-rich and the middle class who just don't care. To these people, a hundred bucks in a mutual fund is way better than a night out on the town. Frugality is a badge of honor. To them, it feels way better to drive a 12 year old Chevy that's paid for than a leased European luxury car that will vanish when the lease term is up. It doesn't hurt that the driver of the 12 year old Chevy knows he or she could buy a European luxury car outright. Cash. There comes a point where most people destined for prosperity view the thrill of being a few hundred dollars closer to their goal as superior to the very fleeting pleasure material objects bring. For these folks, money is much more about security than the illusory happiness sold by Madison Avenue.

Speaking of security, a need for security is almost universal among self-made rich people. They crave money not so they can show-off a Bentley or a McMansion; they simply value peace of mind more than acceptance by people who don't really matter anyway.

Although it is certainly possible to get rich if you do the right things and start early enough in life, financial independence should be the goal of every person reading this book. In fact, a measure of financial independence will be imperative in the uncertain future facing us.

The world is changing rapidly and unstoppably. The days of a company taking care of their workers for life in exchange for 30 or 40 years of service are long gone. Where once you went into a company, asked the receptionist for an application, filled it out, and maybe had a few words with the supervisor who, if he liked you, told you start Monday, now the hiring process for even menial jobs has largely become a gauntlet to be run. Most jobs are now applied for online. In the event your résumé is not filtered-out by computer software, you may receive the increasingly rare bounceback email saying "We're carefully considering your qualifications, blah, blah, blah." More often you will hear nothing. If you are exceedingly lucky, you will get a job interview. By telephone. If you do well on the phone interview, you may get invited to several more in-person interviews. If you don't do well, you will be lucky if the company notifies you that they've found a more suitable candidate. Should you get the job, congratulations! Welcome to the new corporate world of pay that is much less than it was decades ago in inflation-adjusted terms, the expectation that you will *always* be on call, and the fact that you will be the first to go if the company decides to cut staff. The point of this is that it is no longer a good idea (or even possible in many cases) to tie one's fortunes to a single company. In the not too distant future, many if not most of us will be mercenaries living in a mercenary world. Fully 40% of us will be temps working on a contract basis in 10 to 20 years. This will absolutely require that we uncouple our financial lives from the whims of a single company.

Unless they actually own a company, wealthy people do not put their all their eggs into a single company basket. In fact, some rich people make large annual incomes without having any job at all. While income inequality and wealth inequality have both been very much in the news lately, it's important to understand that they are not the same thing and have only become a problem in recent decades because virtually all the benefits engineered by government have flowed from the bottom to the top.

There should be a certain amount of income inequality. Somebody who puts him- or herself through night school while working full-time or a doctor who does four years of undergraduate work, four years of medical school, and four more years of internship/residency should not be making the same money as someone who pushes a broom. Marx's "from each according to his ability, to each according to his need" not only contradicts human nature, but is patently unfair to the person who works hard for years to develop his or her natural gifts. The problem with income inequality in recent years is that it has become so unashamedly "in your face." If a profitable business gets any kind of subsidies from the taxpayer (especially in the form of public assistance to ill-paid employees) there is no reason an already well-paid CEOs should get bonuses. The arrogant new conventional wisdom amongst some wealthy people that "only" 47% of Americans pay "all" the taxes is not only patently untrue, but a pretty good indication that there will be a lot of clueless Marie Antoinettes out there when and if the social instability that naturally occurs in a country without a middle class ever comes to pass.

Wealth inequality, as opposed to income inequality, is far less cut-and-dried. Should people be allowed to amass wealth? Yes. The reason baseball players make so much more than teachers is that they create immediate value in terms of the revenues they generate. While a teacher may guide the next Einstein, the professional baseball player is bringing people to stadiums which employ thousands and generate millions in tax revenues right now. There are simply many more people who can teach kids how to read than can throw a 100 m.p.h. fastball with control. Fair or not, the laws of supply and demand dictate that the baseball player will make much more money.

The major problems with wealth inequality are a lack of education on how one actually goes about accumulating wealth, a lack of opportunity that has much less to do with funding than the fact that chaos is allowed to reign in some schools, and basic unfairness built into the law by politicians who are always thinking ahead to their own post-Congress careers.

The lack of education is easily remedied for the person with the curiosity and willingness to acquire it. It is very easy (from a knowledge standpoint) to accumulate and grow wealth. Everything you need to know is in the pages that follow this one. Many people who learn how to invest find themselves shocked at how straightforward it really is. It often, in fact, seems as though it should have been obvious with the benefit of hindsight. Similarly, it took thousands of years of medicine for humankind to make the connection between germs and disease. Such is the nature of wealth-building. What is very simple is not so simple when it hasn't yet been discovered.

The lack of opportunity is not nearly so easily addressed. Poverty (the ultimate robber of opportunity) perpetuates itself far more effectively than wealth. Blighted neighborhoods and too remote areas are terrible for business. Though money can fix rundown schools, it cannot fix horrendous learning environments and frequently uninvolved parenting. Companies pay as little as possible (often to their own detriment) not because they are hanging on by a thread, but simply because they can. All those who lament the well-paid manufacturing jobs of the past and feel that it is somehow only right that "mindless" service sector jobs should pay so miserably should keep in mind that it really was no harder to turn a screw on an assembly line than to scoop a basket of fries out of the fryer. One huge advantage rich people have over poor people is that they value education and have the ability to pay for it. They understand the nexus between education and financial success far more than poor, working-, and middle class people. I do not fault them for placing a high value on education; I fault the parents and educational system in this country that have not only failed miserably to prepare kids for higher education, but have basically ensured wealth inequality by letting the costs of higher education inflate out of the reach of all but the wealthy. If enough parents had simply said "no" to tuition increases used to fund swimming pools and seven figure salaries for football coaches and college presidents, their money would have eventually talked.

Tax policy is another factor that reinforces wealth inequality. The income cutoff for Social Security tax is $113,700. The argument that, since there are upper limits to what one can collect there should be limits on what is withheld, is spurious at best. People who die young get essentially nothing. People who live to be 115 collect until they die. Social Security is one of those things that shows just how much an "us versus them" mentality has taken root in this country. The idea that we are now a country of "makers" and "takers" shows just how far we've descended since World War II when poor Kansas farm boys fought alongside Yale undergrads because, despite their differences, they were countrymen. Maximum long-term capital gains rates are capped at 20%, even for billionaires. Qualified dividends are, likewise, capped at 20%. The argument here is that if rich people had to pay ordinary tax rates they wouldn't invest or hold stocks for the long-term. This is also a spurious argument. With certificate of deposit rates less than one percent it's doubtful investors would forego 9.4% average annual returns out of spite.

By now, many of the people reading this have concluded that I must be some kind of anti-American socialist. I'm not. America is neither capitalist nor socialist, but has a mixed economy. Unfortunately, we have skewed towards unfettered capitalism in recent decades. I am no great fan of taxes, particularly when the money is wasted as it so often is, but there should at least be the perception of fairness. Perhaps we should be asking ourselves why people in nominally "socialist" countries with far lower degrees of wealth inequality are so much happier. Scandinavians pay far higher tax rates than we do, yet have a higher standard of living. In answer to the "truism" that "socialism makes everyone poor," I have to wonder why Scandinavia has so many billionaires. There has been much talk of a "skills gap" in the United States in recent years.

Thomas K Lamb

This is where companies have positions that go unfilled because there are no qualified candidates to do the job. Alas, there is no skills gap. There is only an attempt by some companies to defy the ironclad laws of economics. There are plenty of people out there with five years' experience and sufficient education in machining, but a definite shortage of people with five years' experience and sufficient education in machining willing to work for ten bucks an hour.

Rich people no doubt enjoy certain advantages. Whether they are fair or unfair advantages is irrelevant. They exist because the laws, in large part, have made them exist. Life is not fair. Those who waste their lives waiting for fairness will be inevitably disappointed. Though there are some advantages rich people have that the rest of us could never hope to exploit, there are ways an average person can build wealth by taking the same advantages rich people do. This is the entire premise of this book. The key to wealth is to follow the money, that is, to do the things rich people do that make and keep them rich.

To really understand why things are the way they are and where they're likely to go from here, it pays to have a basic understanding of economics. Economics is not, contrary to popular belief, about money. Economics is about making choices in conditions of scarcity. Anything that people actually want (including, or especially, money) is scarce. Clean air, drinkable water, and land are all scarce. Good jobs are certainly scarce. Opportunity cost, that is, what you give up in order to choose something else, is central to economics. This is why we end up where we do in life based mostly on the choices we make. Everything has an opportunity cost. The choice to go to college comes at the cost of money you might make by getting a full-time job right out of high school. The choice to enroll in a 401(k) comes at the cost of money you could have in your paycheck right now. The cost of going out on a date with a super model or the world's most eligible bachelor comes at the cost of time you might have spent reading this book!

Unfortunately, we find ourselves living in a time of structural economic change. These periods in history, while ultimately driving living standards higher, always come at great cost to some. Although some letter writers to the editor and Internet message board posters like to blame outsourcing and free trade *entirely* for the current plight of the American worker, the real problem (or economic benefit depending on your point of view), is technology. The American worker undoubtedly now competes directly with workers from India and China in the world market, but what has really caused the high-paying manufacturing jobs of the past to rapidly disappear is technology. One robot can now do the work of 100 humans with no breaks, no fringe benefits, and no work-life balance issues. Companies don't forego technology solely to create jobs. They never have. This increased productivity is great for shareholders, but devastating for those workers replaced by machines.

In the past "creative destruction," that process where new technologies replace old things or ways of doing things, has always eventually benefitted everyone. When kerosene lamps were replaced with incandescent light bulbs, everyone suddenly had ample light to do things at night (such as reading without eyestrain) they couldn't do before. When people left the farms to work in factories they eventually got 40 hour work weeks, better pay that further fueled American economic growth, and a far higher standard of living.

The problem facing us today is that, where increasing productivity always resulted in higher real incomes for everybody in the past, this trend has not continued with the explosion in technological innovation that started in the 1990s. While we can now call long distance practically for free, paychecks have, if anything, shrunk dramatically in inflation-adjusted terms. Part of the reason for this is the law of supply and demand. If machines can do the work of more people more cheaply (and with less drama), there is no reason for companies to hire any more people than are absolutely necessary to operate and maintain the machines. If there is a surplus of labor, the cost of that labor will be cheaper than if there is a shortage.

Everything would be dandy if the British economist John Maynard Keynes' predictions had come true. Back in the thirties he predicted that, due to productivity gains, the average workweek would be 16 hours by the year 2000. It was not an unreasonable guess. Ninety-six hour workweeks in sweatshops or on the farm had been a reality in his lifetime. What he didn't consider is that Britain and the United States would become consumer societies where what had once been luxuries would become necessities. Consumption now accounts for 70% of the American economy.

The simple (and probably only) solution to our rapidly eroding standard of living would be for companies to just pay more. Unfortunately, this would be reliant on altruism which is perhaps the rarest commodity of them all in this world. Despite the fact that companies are hoarding vast quantities of cash (with the somewhat valid excuse that government regulation is causing uncertainty), punitive taxation is probably not a good solution. This would *in fact* result in cases where success was being punished (a conservative rallying cry for their constituency having to pay *any* taxes).

The average person is certainly not blameless for the economic condition we find ourselves in today. The same people that rail against big box stores who "exploit their workers" are often the first people to show up to get a deal. Though many lament that these heartless stores have ruined Thanksgiving by forcing their employees to work, they are often the first ones there once the leftover turkey has been hastily thrown into the refrigerator. People talk about how unpleasant it is to be jammed into a flying cigar tube with no free meals, snacks, or blankets provided, but expect to pay next to nothing for their flight to Disney World. The only thing that could possibly change all this (and that will almost certainly not happen) is if people voted with their wallets. If people spent their money at the Costcos of the world instead of those retailers who give low prices at the expense of their employees, things might change. If a fast food chain let it be known that their employees were an important resource (and treated accordingly), they would certainly have my business even if the hamburger cost 64 cents more. Ironically, American business, now addicted to cost-cutting as if revenues hardly mattered, would in many cases profit handsomely by paying more. People who work at discount stores tend to shop at discount stores. People who work at fast food restaurants tend to eat at fast food restaurants. There is a thing in economics called "goodwill." This is an intangible asset some companies have that give them a competitive advantage over their rivals. It seems almost crazy to me that only a relative handful of companies have decided to acquire this tremendously cheap asset.

Sadly, things will most likely not change. Once bad habits are formed, they're very hard to get rid of. We will continue to be a consumer society that buys solely on price. Companies will continue to meet our demands at the lowest possible cost. You can't change the world, but you can change yourself.

Enough pontificating. The rest of this book is concerned with the nuts and bolts of building a prosperous life. So far in this introduction I have used terms such as "stocks," "bonds," and "mutual funds" in the way many financial writers use them: with the seeming assumption that you already know what these things are. While many people are familiar with these terms, many don't really know what they are. There is no shame in this. If you've never been taught something you could not possibly be expected to know it. I will explain further in the text what these things are in detail. For now, suffice it say that they are very powerful wealth-building tools, the tools with which many a fortune has been constructed. They are the tools you will be using.

Of all the things rich people do that grow and perpetuate their wealth, none is more important than education. Education need not be of the formal variety to benefit you greatly. The aim of this book is to give you a complete and useful education in personal finance and how rich people get that way, at a very nominal cost. This book will also contain a chapter on getting an edge in life. Much of that edge concerns educating yourself. This does not necessarily mean going to an Ivy League university. In fact, it does not necessarily mean going to a university at all. It's important to understand that despite what a politician, a media pundit with an agenda, a bitter colleague, or a discouraged family member might say, your future is firmly in your hands. Though there are some truly evil rich and powerful people out there, none can possibly influence the outcome of your life as much as you can. Though hating the rich (particularly the arrogant clueless ones) has become something of a national pastime in the wake of the Great Recession, jealousy is not admirable trait. It's far better to live by the maxim: If you can't beat them, join them.

I
Taking Stock

If you want to get to where you want to go, it's best to know where you are. Taking stock of yourself is a great first step on the long road that leads to prosperity. Not only is it a useful part of the preparation process that immediately precedes execution, but is also a buffer zone between the old paycheck to paycheck life you may have been living your entire adult life and your new life of eventual financial independence. If "failure to plan is planning to fail," the taking stock process is where the foundations of a plan are first laid.

As simple as it sounds, the key to building wealth is to live below your means and to invest the difference. The taking stock process is one that tells you if you are, in fact, living below your means, or if it is even possible to live below your means considering your income and expenses. If you are not living below your means (or are unable to) the self-inventory process is a great starting point for thinking about what changes you will have to make in order to achieve the goals you are probably just now formulating.

It is entirely possible to succeed without taking stock. A recent study found that the most successful cold turkey tobacco quitters are men who quit with absolutely no prior planning whatsoever. These are men who run out of cigarettes one day and never get around to going to the store to buy another pack. Just diving into an endeavor is often enough to make it work. Companies are discovering that automatically enrolling their new employees in a retirement savings plan (thus forcing them to opt-out if they don't want to participate) yields far better results than requiring the employee to be proactive. Such is the power of inertia.

For most people, however, taking stock and making a plan are often the first ingredients of eventual success. Although it's possible to succeed as an investor with little or no preplanning, the financial aspect of one's life is, in most cases, best approached as a business. If your life is your business, then you are the CEO of that life (as corny as that may sound). To be the CEO makes you captain of the ship, master of your own destiny, and key stakeholder in the entire enterprise. Most people look at a politician or a business "leader" at some point and think: "I could do a lot better than that guy." Being the CEO of your own life gives you the chance to prove it, if only to yourself.

Unlike an investing regimen, starting a business absolutely requires planning. Capital must be secured, a market analysis must be done, licenses and permits have to be applied and paid for, lawyers have to be consulted. The bigger the business the more complicated it gets. It takes effort and money. Many a small business person has doomed his or her aspirations right from the start by skimping on things critical to what might have culminated in success. Where a rich person would see hiring a good attorney as an investment, many small business owners have learned the hard way that legal advice gleaned for free on the Internet was worth exactly what they paid for it.

Happily, although you should put no less effort into the planning for your future success than those starting businesses do, you, unlike them, need not spend much money at all. Good financial advice can be had cheaply or for free in the library or on the Internet (with the caveat that there is a lot of bad advice out there as well). While it's true that rich people will (very wisely) pay big money for financial advisors and accountants, you will not need to think about this until you are well on your way to affluence. It *will* happen, just not yet. There are no liability issues involved with investing in corporations. Unlike a small service business where the sole proprietor is on the hook if something goes wrong, shareholders in corporations do not assume any personal liability. If you buy stock in a pharmaceutical company and the company gets sued, you may lose your investment in that particular company but you won't lose your house.

It's best not to spend too much time planning. The biggest problem people have in changing any facet of their lives is execution. It would actually be far better in the long run to execute without planning than to plan ad infinitum without execution. Most working people who aspire to financial independence should plan for precisely one month.

One month is exactly how long it takes to really know if you are living at, above, or below your means. A common (and profoundly useful) exercise financial planners recommend is to track every single penny that comes in and goes out for an entire month. I recommend that this be done in a pocket memo book with a pen in real time rather than on a device with a receipt after you get home. The few seconds spent writing down a purchase is a few seconds you have to think about whether or not that purchase was really necessary.

It's critically important that you not try to fool yourself. Don't brown bag your lunch every day of this month if you normally eat out twice a week. Don't cook a meal for your significant other on Saturday night if you ordinarily go out. There will be plenty of time to change your spending habits later; for now, just spend the way you always do. Make sure you record every single purchase. A pack of gum is as vital to this experiment as a car payment. Don't run around the house turning off lights in an effort to reduce your electric bill. Don't volunteer for overtime if you generally don't. Make this month as typical of a month in your life as possible.

Some people will be disheartened by this experiment. Many of those who thought they were just getting by (or worse) will find they were correct. Some will find that, though they indulge themselves from time to time, they are not willing to give up the dinners and lunches out that make life bearable to them. A significant number of people will find themselves shocked at how much money they let slip through their fingers.

Advertisers have long known the power of pointing out that something or other costs "just pennies a day." Human psychology rarely prompts us to add-up all those "pennies a day." When we do, however, we are invariably surprised. This exercise not only shows us where we stand financially, but is a good demonstration of how our own psychology can be put to work either for or against us.

We humans are masterful at kidding ourselves. Most of us think we're pretty good with money. This exercise forces us to be honest; the numbers do not lie. Some of us are, in fact, pretty good with money, but many of us are not nearly as frugal as we thought.

For those who discover that they could be allocating their money much more wisely (and who are ready, willing, and able to execute) the next question is *how* to invest.

The obvious choice for those with substantial consumer debt would seem to be paying-down credit card balances. From a strictly financial standpoint, this is an absolute no-brainer. With average credit card rates of 13.02% there is simply no better investment than paying-down credit card debt. Not only is this equivalent to getting a *guaranteed* 13.02% return on your investment, but it's a guaranteed 13.02% *tax-free* return on your investment. With historical rates of return just over 9% in the stock market, paying down credit card debt is the obvious choice. Or is it?

There are many financial pundits out there who stress paying-off debts before doing anything else. On the surface this makes perfect sense. A guaranteed tax-free 13.02% return beats a 9.4% (usually taxable) return any day of the week. The math is indisputable. There is only one problem with this. Of all the things in this world that can be financed, retirement isn't one of them.

It is theoretically possible for a person with huge personal debts to spend decades whittling-down their debts only to end up penniless. They might start out with a huge negative net worth and end up with a less huge negative net worth. It's a negative net worth all the same. You can't eat a lesser negative net worth in retirement. While there is a moral argument to be made about paying debts, it does neither society nor the person who owes large sums of money any good to live in grinding poverty in old age because he or she spent a lifetime paying down debt.

I am in favor of a balanced solution. First and foremost, I advocate signing-up for a company retirement plan the first day you can. The 401(k) (or 403(b) for people who work for non-profits) is a retirement savings plan offered by most companies. The money deducted from the employee's paycheck is usually tax-deferred (except in the case of the still rare Roth 401(k)), often comes with a company match (the only free money in the universe), and is protected from creditors by law. Many people find the array of investment choices offered in their 401(k)s dizzying, but those choices can always be changed. The beauty of the 401(k) plan is twofold: It's an easy way to get started on the road to financial independence and it harnesses the immense power of inertia because the investments are automatically deducted without any need to be proactive.

With the possible exception of a reasonable emergency fund, all other money available and earmarked for investment should go towards paying-off consumer debt. Most wealthy people have taxable investment accounts (in addition to retirement accounts), but are usually not burdened with the same types of debts regular people are. Taxable investment accounts are one way in which many rich people expand and perpetuate their wealth, but maxing-out a 401(k) and getting rid of high interest consumer debt should always take precedence. Even financial advisors hired by the wealthy direct their clients to fund a retirement plan and get rid of "bad" debt before funding a taxable investment account.

While not absolutely necessary, taking stock of oneself is beneficial for most people who aspire to financial independence. Not only does an honest self-assessment often provide a simplified roadmap to the future, but a window to the past. Many people who go on to achieve financial success recall the period in which they took stock of themselves as a crossroads in their lives. The road to affluence is as much about the journey as the destination. Just seeing how far you've come is often the thing that motivates you to keep going.

Chapter One Takeaways

- Taking stock of yourself is a great, albeit not absolutely necessary, way to begin your journey to eventual financial independence.

- Tracking your expenses for an entire month is a great way to find out where you stand.

- Be honest with yourself!

II

Start!

It is impossible to overstate the importance of execution. Time is as important to your eventual financial freedom as the amount of money you put into investments, if not more so. Compounding is the thing that turns small amounts of money invested regularly over years and decades into sometimes vast fortunes.

Six percent of a $30,000 a year salary invested at a very reasonable six percent rate of return will yield $142,304.74 after 30 years. This assumes no raises. If you factor in a 50% match on the first six percent of salary saved (a very common company match formula), you will have $213,457.10 after 30 years. Adding an additional one percent when you do receive a raise (hopefully each year) will have a dramatic multiplier effect on this figure. Suppose you graduate from college or a trade apprenticeship program at age 23 and find a job with a $40,000 a year salary. Suppose you are able to contribute 15% a year over a 40 year career. You will end up with $928,571.79 assuming no raises or company match. There will almost certainly be raises and a company match, however. It is compounding more than anything else that enables regular working people to not only become millionaires, but to do so without having to live like misers.

One dramatic illustration often cited about compounding is that someone saving $2,000 a year from ages 25-35 then stopping will end up with more money at age 65 than someone who saves $2,000 a year from ages 35-65. This is not exactly true, but pretty damn close. Someone who saved $2,000 a year from ages 25-35 (once again assuming a six percent rate of return) then stopped would end up with $151,401.53 at age 65. The person who contributed $2,000 a year from ages 35-65 would end with $158,110.03. A $6708.50 difference is pretty small considering one person contributed only $20,000 while the other had to put in $60,000!

Investment returns are far less important in the beginning of an investment program than actually getting started and contributing as much as possible. Some people are very intimidated by having to make investment decisions in a new 401(k). Bad choices are way better than no choices. In 2008, as the Great Recession raged like a hurricane, some people lost up to 40% of their money. For people nearing retirement and those who had locked in their losses in the throes of panic the results were devastating. Million dollar 401(k) balances dropped to $600,000. People with far less comfortable balances saw their retirement prospects evaporate. For young investors, however, it was a once in a century opportunity to buy at ridiculously cheap prices. Who really cared that a $2,000 401(k) balance dropped to $1,200? That $800 would be easily made up. The important (and profitable) thing in this situation was that the investor keep going. Once started and the power of inertia firmly in control, many did.

Some people, drowning in credit card debt, will decide to begin their journey to prosperity by digging out. There is nothing wrong with this. For those psychologically able to see the positive in a negative number, a shrinking credit card balance can be a powerful motivator. That it makes sense from a financial perspective is just the gravy on the mashed potatoes.

Here too, it is imperative to start. One of the insidious things about credit cards is that it is very easy to confuse a low minimum payment with what is really owed. This is by design. In the same way people get rich incrementally, credit card companies are content to make their money piecemeal. Perhaps it's just human nature, but many people will see a $3,000 debt as just a $30 a month bill. Once the minimum payment is made, it's not unusual for people to add on to the debt with the justification that they can surely afford to pay $32 next month.

Unless you are in real trouble, making only the minimum payment cannot really be viewed as progress. This is why I advocate enrolling in a 401(k) even if you are only able to afford to make the minimum payments on consumer debt. Of course, it is absolutely mandatory to make at least the minimum payment.

Credit, as will be discussed in a later chapter, is a wealth-building weapon used by the rich with great effect.

For those who choose to attack debt with a vengeance, nevertheless, the rewards can be greater than any other approach to prosperity. Thirteen percent tax-free beats 9.4% taxable hands down. Not ironically, people who successfully retire large debts often go on to become highly successful investors. This is because, though they might not use inertia in attacking their debt, they have already proven that they can overcome that type of inertia that defeats so many others.

A few people will choose to begin on the path to financial independence by establishing an emergency fund. With interest rates below one percent this is not what the financial pundits would recommend if you have any credit card debt whatsoever, but if it's the thing that works for you it's a good thing. Remember, execution is all that matters for right now. As long as it's done, there is no wrong way to do it.

Just as some people like to shake coffee cans full of coins, some people like to look at bank statements. A thousand dollars to someone who has never saved anything before is a hugely powerful incentive to keep it going.

Momentum is a massive component in investor psychology that cannot be over-stressed. Although saving money in a liquid (easy to get at) vehicle will cause some people to fail because they just cannot resist the temptation to spend money they may never have had before, others will ride the momentum forward. Reaching financial milestones is like nothing else. Watching a hundred dollars turn into a thousand, then two, is often the only reinforcement a person needs to reach escape velocity. Escape velocity is that point where there is no turning back, where financial success becomes a matter of when, not if. If putting money away in a savings account is the catalyst that starts this process, fine. It doesn't matter if you fly, take the train, or drive to your destination as long as you get there.

Like 401(k) and 403(b) investments, saving in a liquid account is best done automatically. Not only is there that old inertia thing again, but it doesn't pay to obsess over savings and investments because checking balances too often is like watching a clock. Your time horizon isn't days and weeks, but years and decades. Checking balances too frequently has the effect of making progress feel too slow. Impatience is the enemy of the successful investor.

Most companies will allow you to divert a portion of your pay to your savings account. If your company doesn't, most banks will be happy to debit regular savings deposits from your checking account. Internet banks are a good option for your emergency fund. Most pay higher interest rates than brick-and-mortar banks and have low minimum initial deposits without fees.

Whichever avenue you choose, start as soon as possible. There will inevitably be some people who conclude that they're too old to start or that they can only spare five bucks a week. Start anyway. Something is always better than nothing. The bull market of the 1990s made many people a lot of money despite the fact that they could only afford to make modest contributions. A decade of outsized investment returns can have a gigantic impact on your investment portfolio. While there is no guarantee that you will get rich contributing only small amounts, it's virtually assured that you will have nothing if you contribute nothing.

Start!

Chapter Two Takeaways

- Execution is the most important thing you can do right now.

- It doesn't matter *how* you save or invest, just that you start!

- You're never too old or young to start.

- Something always beats nothing.

III

What These Things Are

As mentioned earlier, a 401(k) is a company sponsored retirement plan named for the section of the U.S. tax code where it was buried for years before some bureaucrat discovered it and companies realized it was better than finding bags of gold hidden in the warehouse. At long last those pesky defined-benefit (traditional) pension plans could be replaced by defined-contribution plans and all the responsibility for employees' retirements shifted from the company to the employees. It was a win-win for American business, an unqualified disaster for the American worker. Even the guy who found it amidst the thousands and thousands of pages of rules and regulations has conceded that it has been an utter catastrophe. Where once American workers largely enjoyed retirement security, retirement has become as insecure as every other facet of American life over the past 30 years.

For as much of a dud as the 401(k) is, it's all most of us have to work with. While most people do far worse with a 401(k) than with a defined-benefit pension, there are a relatively few people who come out way ahead. The reason for this is that *every* ingredient necessary to achieve wealth is contained in all but the worst 401(k)s.

Nearly all 401(k)s offer a menu of mutual funds. Mutual funds are pools of money used to buy financial instruments. Your weekly contribution is combined with millions of others to buy large amounts of stocks, bonds, REITs, or commodities. Mutual funds can be actively managed or passive. Actively managed mutual funds typically come with higher management fees. (The people who administer these mutual funds are paid with fees lopped-off your returns.

These fees vary widely and bear watching. Oddly, mutual funds are the one item that seems to defy the rule of thumb that you get what you pay for. Cheaper mutual funds tend to outperform more expensive ones!) Passive (or "index") funds are mutual funds that replicate an existing index such as the S&P 500 or the Dow 30 that economists use to measure overall market performance. They are called passive funds because, unlike actively managed funds where a team of analysts must research and choose investments, the index fund manager simply buys and holds proportionate amounts of every stock or bond in the index. Whoever invented the mutual fund was absolutely brilliant. Not only did this invention open up the investment world to the common person, but each share (which can contain fractional percentages of hundreds or even thousands of different stocks) provides instant diversification that goes a long way towards minimizing risk.

Stocks should be at the heart of any investment portfolio. Stocks (a.k.a. securities, a.k.a. equities) are the tool with which many of the wealthy have gotten that way. Stocks are units of ownership in a publicly traded (meaning it trades on a stock exchange) company. When you own a stock you literally own a piece of the company. This does not entitle you to free stuff if the stock is in Walmart, Macy's, or McDonald's, but it does entitle you to a share in the company's fortunes. Individual stocks (as opposed to stocks held within mutual funds) come with voting rights. Though you do not get to decide how much the CEO makes, you can vote to fire the board of directors who do.

Many companies pay dividends. Dividends are your (the owner's) share of the profits. They are most often paid quarterly or at the end of the year. Sometimes a "special dividend" is declared. Dividends are a major factor in building wealth. Reinvested dividends, that is, using the proceeds of a dividend to buy more shares in the company or mutual fund, results in a snowball effect. The reinvested dividends from the stocks in your mutual funds will, at a point, account for a larger portion of your growing 401(k) balance than your paycheck deductions!

Not all companies pay dividends. This is not necessarily a bad thing. Some companies plow "retained earnings" back into the business. If you own a highly successful retail store, for example, the board may decide to use the profits to open more locations, thus earning even more profits. Berkshire Hathaway, the legendary investor Warren Buffett's company, has only ever paid a dividend once and has never split. (A stock split is where a stock trading at, say, $100 a share will be split into two shares at $50 apiece. This is done to make the stock more affordable to individual investors.) In 1965 Berkshire Hathaway was trading at $18 a share. Today it trades for more than $175,000 for a single share!

Stocks are divided into groups based on market capitalization. This is relevant because you will see terms such as "large-cap," "mid-cap," and "small-cap" among the menu choices in your 401(k).

Large-cap companies are, as the name implies, the biggest, most well-known companies. With market capitalizations over $200 billion, this group contains those stocks known as "blue chip" stocks. These are companies that have usually been around for a long time and are financially healthy. Most pay a good dividend. This means that, even if they temporarily go down in value in a market swoon, you will be paid to wait for them to come back up. Some examples of large-cap companies are Apple, Chevron, Starbucks, and Mastercard.

Mid-cap companies have market capitalizations of anywhere between $10 billion and $200 billion. Many of these companies are also household names. Applied Materials, Southwest Airlines, and Hess are all mid-cap companies. A lot of these companies also pay healthy dividends.

It's important to understand the correlation between risk and reward in investing. The smaller the market capitalization of a stock, the more volatile it will be. Mid-caps are riskier than large-caps, but have a potential for higher returns. This is why economics, while all about choice, is so pertinent to money. By buying smaller capitalization stocks you give up some safety for possible gain. The reason for this is that smaller capitalization stocks have more room for growth than well-established blue chips. Large-cap stocks, on the other hand, offer a margin of safety because they normally have large stockpiles of cash with which to weather an economic storm.

Small-caps are stocks with market caps between $250 million and $2 billion dollars. These are far riskier than large- and mid-cap stocks, but have historically outperformed them as a group. Some pay dividends; many don't. Though there a lot of companies you've never heard of within this group, there are some companies that are well-known. Jack in the Box, Lennox International, and Treehouse Foods are all small-cap stocks.

Micro-cap stocks are the riskiest of all. With market caps below $250 million, these are the stocks with which you can hit a home run or (far more likely) lose your money. Any portion of your portfolio allocated to micro-cap stocks should be small. In fact, you really don't need them unless you have a gambling itch that needs to be scratched from time to time. You can win big with micro-caps, but there is a reason that some stocks cost $100 a share and others cost just five cents.

There are a ton of urban legends out there about money in general and stock investing in particular. Your co-worker's brother-in-law *did not*, in fact, make millions by buying Walmart for two bucks a share in 1972. (Walmart was *never* two bucks a share.) That girl you went to elementary school with *did not* have a sorority sister who later made a billion dollars by buying Chuck's Pharmaceuticals just before Chuck discovered the cure for tennis elbow in his garage. Many of the charlatans in the financial realm get rich by selling the illusion of quick money through trading "penny stocks." (Penny stocks are often "cheap for a good reason" stocks that usually fit into the micro-cap category. Not all micro-cap stocks or stocks trading under $10 a share are shady, however.) One of the most nefarious scams is the "pump and dump" scheme. Hucksters will buy large quantities of stocks that trade for mere cents, flood Internet message boards with rumors that the company is about to release something big, wait for the gullible to pile-in, then sell right before the whole thing collapses.

Although it's theoretically possible that some tiny pharmaceutical company trading for a dollar a share could get FDA approval for a cancer drug and go up 1,000% overnight, more fortunes are made by hitting the lottery than in this manner. Many people live under the misconception that, since risk and reward have a correlation, it's necessary to take big risks in order to enjoy big rewards. This is simply not true despite what the infomercial guys say. Warren Buffett, indisputably the greatest stock investor of all time, did not get rich buying speculative companies. He got rich buying Coca-Cola, American Express, Dairy Queen, and Geico Insurance. Moreover, he did not get rich trading into and out of the market; he held his stocks for decades (and still does). Unlike the day traders and stock trading "system" peddlers (none of whom you've ever heard of), Warren Buffett's optimum holding period for a stock is "forever." The point here is that you can do very well holding "boring" stocks and avoiding excessive risk.

As if all this information wasn't enough, there are two main investing styles (and, subsequently, stock mutual funds tailored to suit the investor's preference).

Value investing is where the investor or fund manager looks for stocks trading at a discount to their intrinsic value. A stock can be undervalued by the market for a variety of reasons. An ultimately sound company might be dealing with lawsuits related to a defective product. Earnings for a single quarter might have come in below analyst's expectations. In the 1990s when technology stocks were all the rage, some companies were undervalued simply because they were unexciting. It was easy to forget that people still needed toothpaste and roofing shingles when all these amazing gadgets were coming onto the market. It's important to understand that the share price of a stock is not necessarily a reflection of its value. Apple at $400 a share is dirt cheap. A semiconductor company at $10 a share can be massively overvalued. The value investor looks for the stock whose real value is unrecognized by the market. Warren Buffett's career has been the *magnum opus* of value investing. If value investing is your style, it pays to bear in mind that rich people don't hesitate to pay for expertise. Unless you have tons of time and detailed knowledge of the metrics that go into determining what a stock is really worth, hiring an expert is a smart move. Happily, this is exactly what you're doing when you invest in an actively managed value stock mutual fund.

Growth investing is an investing style where the investor or fund manager buys stocks he or she thinks will keep going up. The old saying that "what goes up must come down" may hold true in the long run, but frequently doesn't in the short run. Many individual investors experience the singular disappointment of taking their profits on a stock that is on a tear only to see the stock price keep rising after they've sold it. Growth fund managers don't necessarily look for cheap stocks. A company whose stock price has gone up due to the release of a hot product may make even more money when the upgraded product comes out. Growth investing is sometimes called "momentum investing." It's important to point out that many growth stocks don't pay dividends. Many executives of growth-oriented companies by their very nature are inclined to put retained earnings back into the company rather than pay dividends in order to make the company grow even more.

Of the two styles, value has done better than growth over the long haul. You can make money either way, nonetheless. Many people find that boring (think stodgy value stocks) is more suitable to their risk tolerance. Growth, on the other hand, is more likely to give you an adrenaline rush when you open your 401(k) statement after a particularly exciting quarter. Whichever your preferred style, your 401(k) menu offerings will provide guidance with fund names such as "Mid-cap Value" or "Small-cap Growth." Though I lean towards value investing, a blend of the two styles will normally serve you well.

In addition to large-cap, mid-cap, small-cap, value, and growth, there are other types of funds you may find in your menu of 401(k) options. Commodity or "natural resources" funds invest in things like oil, gold, potash, lumber, and wheat. "Precious metals" funds are more specific to silver, gold, platinum, and palladium. They may invest in the actual metals themselves, or buy stocks in the companies that mine these resources.

REITs are real estate investment trusts. They own things such as office buildings, apartment communities, nursing homes, hospitals, and resorts. Not quite the same sort of pure real estate play as homebuilder or land development stocks, investing in REITs is akin to being a landlord (minus the nightmare tenants). They may not appreciate in value like a go-go growth stock, but they usually provide a reliable income stream. Just a word to my growth investing friends out there: there is nothing wrong with getting rich with income!

Finally, everything I wrote here about stocks pertains not only to American stocks, but to foreign stocks as well. Up until very recently, American investors have for the most part avoided buying stocks of foreign companies. This "home bias" could easily be justified in the past. American markets simply kicked ass while foreign markets came with political instability, currency risk, and illiquidity (that is, it was often hard to find a buyer if you wanted to sell your foreign stocks). American companies with overseas markets and operations gave their investors a little piece of the foreign action at any rate, with very little additional risk.

Things have changed. Drastically. Now fully 60% of the stock market action occurs outside the United States. The demographics of the world are changing in ways that, while good for some countries and not so good for others such as Italy and Japan with vanishing populations, are opening up worlds of opportunity for the investor willing to venture beyond his or her own shores.

New middle classes are springing up in countries like Brazil, Mexico, China, Chile, Ghana, Nigeria, Estonia, Russia, Kuwait, and Vietnam. The middle class is *always* the primary driver of economic growth, anywhere in the world. As formerly poor people begin to get discretionary income and no longer struggle merely to survive, they eat better, buy televisions and automobiles, travel, and save money in banks. The companies that provide the goods and services these newly affluent people demand are poised to do well for decades to come.

The benefits of international investing are immense and proven. When the Great Recession hit the United States and Europe with a vengeance in 2008, many companies in the developing world did just fine. With good governance by formerly corrupt governments, healthy company balance sheets as a result of not having participated in the risky schemes that fueled the Great Recession in the United States, and young, innovative populations, the entire polarity of the world seemed to shift. The expression "When America sneezes, the world catches a cold" no longer seemed to apply. Though it was inevitable that the effects of the Great Recession would be felt everywhere to some degree or other in an interconnected world, some countries did better than others. So too did the investors in the companies of these countries.

Home bias is much like other components of investor psychology in that, while giving the illusion of safety, it ultimately hurts us. Wealthy people (often on the advice of financial advisors) are far more likely to invest abroad than the average amateur investor. Part of the reason for this is that they have more money to risk. The main reason, however, is that rich people most often get that way by running against the herd.

As in so many other ways, "common sense" or "conventional wisdom" is often actually just the opposite. Investing a portion of your stock portfolio in foreign companies actually *reduces* risk and boosts returns.

Any financial advisor worth his or her salt will tell you that diversifying is the single best strategy for managing risk. Holding a mixture of stocks, bonds, and cash, while holding down returns when one asset class is soaring, ensures that you won't lose all your money when markets in one particular asset class tank. Holding different classes of investments such as large-, mid-, and small-cap stocks further reduces risk. Foreign stocks should definitely be part of any diversification strategy.

One of the misconceptions many nervous investors have about foreign stocks is that they are investing in unknown entities. Though sometimes true (especially in the realm of foreign small- and mid-cap stocks), many of the companies in a foreign stock portfolio are, like their large-cap American counterparts, well known household names. Think of how many foreign brands are used by you or by people you know. Honda, Hyundai, Electrolux, Toyota, Nokia, Samsung, Volkswagen, and Ikea are all foreign companies, but we don't usually think of them as being unstable. They're not. America does not have a monopoly on good companies.

Some investors shun foreign companies because they feel they get a big enough bang for the buck (and less risk, even if it's only the perception of extra safety) by buying American blue chips. There is a certain logic in this. One of the benefits (and risks) of global trade is in how currency is exchanged. We hear the terms "weak dollar" or "strong euro" on the news, but these things are rarely explained. A dollar is weak if the conversion rate against another currency is unfavorable. A euro is strong if it buys more of a foreign currency when converted. Central banks often like to keep their county's currency weak because it makes their exports cheaper to foreign buyers (who then buy more products from that country with their stronger money) and more expensive for their citizens to buy foreign (imported) products. The way investors benefit from buying stocks of American companies that do business globally is this: Ford sells more cars to Europeans when the euro is strong against the dollar. Europeans are happy because they can buy a better model Ford; American investors are happy because the company they own is selling more product. They are even happier when the strong euros are converted back into (many more) weak dollars and repatriated to the United States. The investors not only make money by selling cars, but even more money because of favorable exchange rates.

Investing in foreign stocks requires more research than investing in U.S. stocks (which is why it's probably better to invest through a good actively managed or index mutual fund), but it's almost a certainty that the slightly higher costs of investing internationally will prove to be money well-spent in the long run. For those who daydream about having bought Berkshire Hathaway for $18 a share or Apple at seven bucks, international investing is the best chance some as yet undiscovered gem lies in your future.

As a result of the natural maturation process, it is very hard for developed countries (or large-cap companies) to grow as fast as their smaller counterparts. A newborn baby will pack on the pounds far faster and more dramatically than a bodybuilder no matter how many protein shakes he drinks a day. GDP (gross domestic product) is how the growth of countries is measured in economics.

The total value of all final goods and services produced in a country in a year, GDP is a measure of how fast an economy is growing. With more than 200 years of economic growth behind us, the United States cannot match growth rates of a country like Botswana because Botswana can cover much more ground simply by catching up. Four percent GDP growth rates in America would result in an absolutely booming economy; seven percent GDP growth rates or more are the norm in China. Many African countries have been experiencing six percent growth rates in recent years. This is a result of better governance and globalization. At consistent 6% GDP growth an economy can go from subsistence to modern in just a few decades. Though we don't often think about it, we are living in times future generations will envy us. Opportunities abound for those bold enough to take advantage of them. An added bonus is that it can be done with a clear conscience. Investment in a developing country helps the people of that country far more than charity or government aid. GDP growth is the tide that raises all boats.

As stated earlier, foreign stocks also come in large-cap, mid-cap, small-cap, and micro-cap varieties. The benefits of investing in large-cap foreign stocks are similar to those of investing in American large-caps. Many pay healthy dividends and are rock-solid companies. Aside from the currency exchange rates that can either help or hurt such investments, foreign and U.S. markets often don't move in tandem. American stocks had a spectacular 2013 at the same time Europe was struggling to emerge from recession. This made it a great time to own U.S. stocks and will probably prove in retrospect to be a good time to have been accumulating European stocks. The mid-, small-, and micro-cap companies of the world run the gamut, but are surely loaded with hidden gold just waiting to be prospected.

In addition to the market capitalization of companies, the financial world classifies countries by their current stage of economic development. Developed markets are countries such as the U.S.A., Japan, Australia, and the countries of Western Europe. These are countries with well-developed economies, well-regulated financial markets, and that most important ingredient for prosperity, the rule of law. (Corruption is the single biggest factor in the perpetuation of poverty. No sane person wants to invest in a country where contracts are meaningless, property can be expropriated by thieving governments, and bribes are just a cost of doing business.) One of the key reasons Africa has been so historically poor is that foreign aid has traditionally been stolen by despots with exactly zero aid going to the people this aid was intended to help. Happily, Africans are demanding more at the same time governments providing aid are attaching strings. It's no coincidence that Scandinavian countries, with the world's lowest rates of corruption, also enjoy the world's highest living standards.

Emerging markets are those countries that are well on their way to broad prosperity. The "BRICs" immediately come to mind when most people think about emerging markets. Brazil, Russia, India, and China are countries that have made amazing strides in economic development in just the past few decades. In 1978 (the year the first economic reforms were implemented) China was an economic backwater. Literally. The area surrounding Shanghai was swampland; today it is filled with glistening skyscrapers. What makes China stand out among the emerging market nations is that it is now the world's second largest economy. There are other emerging market countries besides the BRICs. Mexico, Chile, and Turkey all have burgeoning middle classes. Malaysia, Indonesia, and Thailand are shockingly modern to the visitor with a 1900s mindset. South Korea hardly rates as an emerging market nation at all. It is nearly as modern as Japan in every way.

There is a great "uncoupling" occurring in the emerging world that you can bet the financial advisors who serve the rich are watching closely. You would be wise to watch it (and eventually profit from it) yourself. For many years, emerging market countries were reliant on developed nations for their continued prosperity. China relied on the U.S. to buy manufactured goods. Countries like Argentina, Chile, and Brazil relied on the U.S. and Western Europe to buy food, wine, copper, and oil. There were no domestic markets capable of driving these economies forward in good times and sustaining them in bad. This is changing at breakneck speed. Aside from better governmental policies, one of the reasons emerging market economies did so much better than the U.S.A. and Europe in the Great Recession is that companies in countries such as China, Brazil, and South Korea could sell their products to their own countrymen, newly laden with cash. Companies found they could make money for their shareholders, both foreign and domestic, without being totally reliant on exports. Look for this trend to accelerate. One strange reality not often noted by the media is that the countries we once outsourced our manufacturing to are now having to outsource themselves. As labor gets more expensive in China, manufacturers move to Vietnam. As hourly wages rise in Mexico, factories are being moved to Guatemala. The downsides of globalization are not a uniquely American problem!

The final category of foreign stocks are the so-called "frontier markets." These stocks come with the potential for huge returns over the long haul, but outsized risk in the short run. These are companies based in countries such as Pakistan, Nigeria, Egypt, Algeria, and Bangladesh. The research needed to invest in frontier market stocks is *always* best left to the professionals. Also, it is wise to limit the percentage of your investment portfolio earmarked for frontier market stocks to no more than five percent. Eventually, some of the countries now considered frontier markets will graduate to emerging market status (as countries like Turkey and South Korea graduate to developed market status), but most of these countries still have a long way to go. Still, I am very optimistic. I think in 30 years large swaths of Africa and Asia, and virtually all of Latin America will be on a par with the U.S., Europe, and Oceania. Younger investors should certainly not entirely shun frontier markets.

Stocks are the one ticket to prosperity available to everyone, but used to maximum effect mostly only by the rich. Fear of the unknown is a major reason for this. While many children of the rich grow up talking about stocks at the dinner table, they remain a scary mystery to most working- and middle class people. I hope the preceding paragraphs demystified them at least a little. The important thing to know about stocks is that, aside from giving tax breaks that many people argue are unfair to non-stockholders, they are the only asset class that consistently beats inflation by enough to actually build wealth.

There is a widely-held belief, especially on the part of new and non-investors, that stocks are necessarily risky while cash in the bank is absolutely safe. This is not true. A diversified portfolio of stock mutual funds that includes large-, mid-, and small-cap U.S. stocks, as well as a healthy dose of foreign stocks, is actually far safer than cash over long periods of time. The reason for this is inflation risk.

When I was a kid my father's shady friends used to come around and flash large wads of cash the day after payday to impress me. They did! They were obviously very rich men, despite the fact they hung around my father's friend's auto repair shop and loaded trucks for a living. Who besides a rich man would have a pocket full of hundreds to flash?

I laugh when I look back on my own naivete. These men who drank beer out of brown bottles while replacing the brakes on their wive's cars were anything but rich. I would bet the farm now that all those wads of "hundreds" were probably a single hundred dollar bill wrapped around a bunch of ones. What isn't so funny is that these men almost certainly had no concept of inflation risk and how devastating it really is. I know for a fact they had no idea what stocks were, let alone how they might turn those wads of "hundreds" into lasting financial security.

If there is one hallmark of rich people, it's that they're chronically cash poor. In the days before debit cards came into wide use (and before McDonald's accepted credit cards) a wealthy person was very likely *that* guy, the one who was seemingly always broke and had to borrow the money for two hamburgers, a small fries, and a Coke from his coworkers. He didn't do this to be obnoxious. He always paid his debts promptly. Sometimes he would even pick up the tab for the whole crew lest they stop inviting him out to lunch. Unlike his colleagues, however, he understood that carrying around cash meant his money was not working for him.

Inflation risk is that risk that your money will steadily erode to the point where what used to be a lot of money becomes chump change. Most people understand inflation to a degree, but few really consider the long term effects. At a very tame rate of two percent inflation, what costs a dollar today will cost $1.02 next year. No big deal, right? Well, actually it is. In ten years what used to cost a dollar will cost $1.22. Over a forty year span (the typical working lifetime) the value of a dollar will disintegrate to the extent that it costs $2.21 to buy what a dollar once did. This, of course, assumes that inflation remains steady at a benign rate of two percent. Alas, inflation rates will almost certainly not remain steady at two percent. In December of 1979 inflation was running at 13.29%!

The best illustration I've come up with to wrap my mind around the erosive effects of inflation is my grandfather's house. In 1955 he bought a house on the street where I now live (different house; same style) brand new for $5,000. Today that same house is appraised at $225,000. Suppose he had decided to "play it safe" and bury his $5,000 in the back yard. In 1955 $5,000 bought a very nice house or a car that would *definitely* turn heads. Today, if we, his heirs, dug up that $5,000 we could buy a very low quality used car or possibly pay the points on a mortgage. That's all. Such is the insidious destructive power of inflation. Grandpop's $5,000 has grown into a $225,000 investment. Not bad, but had he invested the money in stocks at an annualized 9.4% return, his $5,000 would now be $1,002,286.78 without having added a penny to his original $5,000.

Bonds are the other major component of the portfolios of rich people and shrewd 401(k) investors. Bonds provide an anchor that generally stabilizes a portfolio. Nearly always less volatile than stock funds, bond funds provide current income at the same time they offer limited growth.

Bonds can best be thought of as a loan you make to an entity for a set period of time, at an agreed upon rate of interest. The entity can be the U.S. Treasury, your state, your town, or a corporation. Unlike the stockholder, the owner of corporate bonds does not own the company. He or she is a creditor. If a company goes belly-up, bondholders get paid before stockholders see a dime.

The biggest determinants of how much a bond pays are the duration of the bond and the credit rating of the issuer. Short-term bonds generally pay a lower "coupon" (interest) rate than long-term bonds because the lender's money can be tied-up for as long as 30 years with some long-term bonds. A "zero coupon" bond is one that works just like the old fashioned savings bonds you may have gotten as gifts when you were a kid. The bond pays no interest, but is sold well below its face value. When the bond matures, face value is paid-out. Credit rating is everything to an entity wishing to issue bonds. If there was one great historical blunder ever committed by the United States Congress, it was in letting the threat of sovereign default (the government not paying its bills) get out of hand in the first week of August 2011. This resulted in a downgrade of U.S. creditworthiness from AAA (outstanding) to AA+ (excellent) by Standard & Poor's (a bond rating agency) on August 5, 2011. Though an "excellent" credit rating doesn't sound bad, the downgrade made it more expensive for the government to borrow and foreign investors to have just a little less faith in the "full faith and credit" of the U.S. government.

High yield bonds, a.k.a. "junk bonds" are something we've all heard about since the 1980s, but many people really don't understand. Junk bonds are issued by corporate entities with spotty credit ratings. These bonds pay a risk premium just as an individual with less than perfect credit would when buying a car. Not all junk bonds are truly junk and guaranteed to go into default. A company may be trying to get back on its feet after a bankruptcy or restructuring. Companies rebuild their credit the same way individuals do: by paying their bills on time and as agreed. Like stocks in frontier markets, junk bonds should only make up a small percentage of your portfolio and should be held exclusively in mutual funds to dilute the risk of an already risky investment.

All bonds, in fact, should be held in mutual funds in my opinion. Individual bonds are not only hard to research, but rarely return enough to make the time spent doing due diligence worth it. The only possible exception to this rule is municipal bonds. Municipal bonds are bonds issued by local governments or quasi-governmental agencies like the Pennsylvania Turnpike Commission or you local water authority. The sole benefit to investing in municipal bonds is that, if you invest in municipal bonds in your home state, they are generally tax-free. This is neither a concern nor a benefit for people investing in tax-deferred vehicles such as a 401(k), and is usually only the best option for people who are already rich.

Like stock mutual funds, bond funds come in many different varieties. Where stock funds are normally categorized by market capitalization, however, bond funds are usually categorized by duration. There are short-term, intermediate-term, and long-term bond funds. Intermediate- and long-term bond funds are self-explanatory, but many people use short-term bond funds as a place to park cash. Not only is the return better, but the additional risks are minimal.

Some bond mutual funds are categorized by the types of bonds they hold. In addition to the aforementioned types of bond funds, there are specialized bond funds such as TIPS (Treasury Inflation-Protected Securities) that guarantee to beat inflation, and "broad market" bond funds that will invest in bonds of varying maturities.

Although considered by many to be less risky than stocks, it's important to understand that bonds come with their own unique risks. Aside from the risk of default, there is something called "interest rate risk" inherent in bond investing.

There is a whole secret world of bond traders out there, men and women who could literally bore you to death if they chose to. They trade long-term bonds for bonds of a shorter duration at the cost of a revised lower coupon rate, or vice versa. The bonds in your mutual funds are being continually churned by these bond traders. One of the key reasons bond traders trade is to minimize interest rate risk.

When interest rates rise, bond yields fall relative to new bonds that are issued. The reason for this is that no one wants a ten-year bond at five percent when the new ten-year bonds yield six percent. In order to get rid of the now lower rate bonds, the bond trader has to sell them for less than face value to make up for the lower coupon rate. With a wide variety of bonds with different maturities and coupon rates, "total market" bond mutual funds are a far better way for the average investor to deal with the ever-present possibility of interest rate risk.

As of the end of 2012, bonds have outperformed stocks for 30 years. This is a once-in-a-thousand-years anomaly! It will almost certainly not happen again! When making investment decisions it's always a good idea to look at the macroeconomic picture. Over the last 30 years we have had several recessions, two of them particularly severe. Interest rates were cut to the bone in an effort to deal with the ensuing economic malaise. They are so low at the time of this writing that there is realistically nowhere for them to go but up. Though one hopes the bubble in bonds that has been inflating with particular intensity in recent years merely deflates (as opposed to popping), stock market-like returns in the bond market are not sustainable. Unfortunately, carnage is always a possibility when the herd rushes either towards perceived easy money or perceived safety.

Although inflation risk is real and potentially disastrous, it doesn't hurt to have a few bucks in the bank. The problem is when you have *all* your bucks in the bank, particularly from a young age.

Rich people don't have the same worries as people who live paycheck to paycheck. A car breakdown will not be the life-altering event for a wealthy person it might be for someone who loses a job because they are no longer able to get there. Rich people don't sweat over the furnace making it through another winter or a kid's co-pay at the doctor's office. The reason for this is that rich people have emergency funds. Where a credit card or a 401(k) hardship withdrawal (God forbid!) might see a less affluent person through an emergency, wealthy people enjoy the advantage of not paying dearly to deal with an emergency or even worrying about the inevitable unforseen event in the first place. Everyone should have an emergency fund, though I fully realize that in this day and age what you *should* have and what you are *able* to have are frequently two different things.

Within a 401(k), most menu options include GICs. These are "guaranteed investment contracts," essentially cash. Many nervous beginners will put all their money into GICs because of the widely-held belief (which you now know better) that cash is absolutely safe. This is not a problem in the beginning. It's only a problem if the money stays in GICs for years as inflation feasts on it. Still, it's not a bad idea to keep some money in GICs so as not to miss out on great unexpected opportunities when they arise. In a year such as 2013 where stocks performed magnificently, it's not a bad idea to book some profits and redirect some money in the hopes that other assets will outperform next year.

Outside a retirement account, cash can take varying forms. Savings accounts and certificates of deposit, while they don't pay much interest, are FDIC insured. Money market mutual funds are instruments that are as close to cash as possible, but pay a little more. These funds are priced at a stable one dollar a share and invest mostly in "commercial paper." Commercial paper is ultra short-term promissory notes issued by corporations. Although money market mutual funds could conceivably go broke and lose you all your money, none ever has. Money market mutual funds are liquid and usually come with check writing privileges.

Cash held in a taxable brokerage account is put into a "sweep" account. This is where money is "swept" from the account to buy investments, then the profits (hopefully) are swept back in when the securities are sold. Sweep accounts pay interest comparable to bank savings accounts.

Everyone has heard the old investing maxim "buy low, sell high." In contrast to the outlandish claims of hucksters peddling market timing "systems," there is actually a way to reliably do this. "Dollar cost averaging" is a method used by many successful investors to "buy cheap and sell dear." Unlike the "top secret systems" offered for just $29.95 on infomercials shown at 3:00 a.m., there is nothing secret about it. Also known as "buy and hold" investing, dollar cost averaging is an automatic process whereby the investor buys more shares of a stock or bond fund when they are cheap, less when they are expensive. This is done by making regular investments of a set dollar amount (such as a weekly 401(k) contribution of $100) no matter what is going on in the markets. Here's how it works: In week one your $100 contribution buys 10 shares of a stock fund trading at $10 a share. In week two the shares fall to eight bucks a share. Now your $100 buys 12.5 shares. (You can absolutely buy fractional shares in a mutual fund for those of you wondering.) In week three shares rise to $12 a share. Now your $100 buys only 8.3 shares. In week four your shares drop back to $11. This $100 contribution gets you 9.09 shares. The cheaper the shares are, the more your $100 buys; the more expensive the shares, the less your $100 buys. You are buying low. (The time to sell high will be when you make regular withdrawals in retirement.)

Buy and hold investing has been disparaged by many "professional" investors (read: day traders) who mockingly call it "buy and hope" and declared dead more times than a killer cyborg in a science fiction movie. The problem for the naysayers is that it works. Dollar cost averaging is one of those elements of investing, like so many others, that proves the tortoise beats the hare every time. Though you would never know it to listen to some of the talking heads on CNBC, Bloomberg, or the Fox Business channel, buy and hold investors beat the vast majority of active traders hands down. By a wide margin.

What the market or an individual stock will do in a given day, week, or month cannot be known with certainty. Though the charlatans trying to separate you from your money on infomercials claim to know *exactly* the right moment to buy or sell a stock, many hedge fund managers and stock traders *imply* that they know. They don't. All they can do is make educated guesses based on technical analysis, by divining charts, and on analyst opinion. Some of these guesses pan out. Many don't. I have seen "strong buy" and "strong sell" opinions for the same stock on the same day from different analysts.

There is only one thing investors can control with certainty. Most investors become aware of this fact soon after they begin to really understand investing. That thing is the price you, the investor, will pay for an investment. You cannot control the weather, but you can take an umbrella with you just in case. Tomorrow's lottery numbers are utterly unknowable. (Incredibly, there are people who actually pay money for "insight" into tomorrow's numbers from "psychics.") It's up to you, however, whether you buy tickets or just save your two bucks.

One of the few things government can be applauded for in the past couple of years is enacting a statutory requirement that fees be disclosed to the 401(k) investor. (Mutual funds have had to disclose fees forever, but 401(k) administrators have historically been very sly about adding hidden fees on top of the mutual fund fees you already pay.) Rich people pay very close attention to what things cost; you should too. A one or two percent difference in cost may not sound like much, but when compounded over years and years these fees add up to astronomical numbers. The investment business being just that—a business—there are other traps out there companies use to increase their bottom lines.

Some mutual funds charge "loads." A load is just a sales commission you pay for the privilege of being allowed to buy shares; there is absolutely no benefit to you whatsoever when you pay a load. Some of these loads are in upwards of five percent! That means you need to make more than five percent above and beyond the fund's other expenses just to break even! Why anyone would ever pay a load is beyond me. With plenty of great funds with no loads and low expenses it's like voluntarily paying $5.75 for what you could get for ten cents. Some load funds with decent rates of return are available to 401(k) investors with the load waived. Find out!

Being a business like any other, mutual fund families try to attract new customers. They do this by advertising. Unfortunately, you, the existing investor, get to pay for this advertising through "12b-1 fees" which is just an IRS-esque term for marketing expenses. Arguably, this is fair. In theory more money in the fund means more choice to the fund manager and possible better returns for the existing shareholders. There is an amazing wrinkle to this, however, that is quite possibly the best example of chutzpah known to man.

Sometimes a mutual fund will close to new investors because there is too much money in the fund. (Yes, too much money is a problem that actually exists in this world.) A small-cap value fund, for instance, may close because the fund manager is unable to find any compelling stocks to buy without deviating from the fund's stated strategy. This is fine. Closing a mutual fund to new investors protects existing investors. What isn't fine is when mutual funds are closed to new investors at the same time 12b-1 fees are being charged to existing investors to advertise a fund that is not open to new investors! This amazing display of audacity, unbelievable as it is, actually happens.

All mutual funds come with what is called an "expense ratio." This is the cost of running a mutual fund. Managers, analysts, the clerks who prepare year-end tax statements, and the people who clean the offices all need to be paid. Expense ratios are deducted from investment returns. Generally, index funds have lower expense ratios than actively managed funds. Funds that require more legwork by analysts will have higher expense ratios. This is fair. A fund manager who has to go traipsing around Pakistan looking for stocks to buy faces obstacles a fund manager who only needs to look up what stocks currently comprise the Russell 2000 index doesn't. As I mentioned earlier, rich people are not afraid to pay for expertise. It's just the cost of doing business. Investing, keep in mind, is a business. It's *your* business. One day you will look back and see how central that business was to the overall enterprise that is your life.

All that being said, cheaper is better. Many times 401(k) menus will contain two nearly identical stock funds with wildly different expense ratios. Unless the five and ten year annualized returns (which will be provided in the fund information) are radically different in favor of the more expensive fund, go with the cheaper option. One irony that is perhaps unique to the investing world is that cheaper is often better not just for the obvious reason, but that it's *qualitatively* better as proven by published annual returns. Vanguard, the fund family known for its cheap funds and literally inventing indexing, destroys many of its far more expensive competitors.

If there is one takeaway I hope the reader gets from this chapter, it's that what you pay for your investments is central to your future success. Parting with illusions (such as the illusion that there is some secret to wealth you might later discover) is often unpleasant, but ultimately empowering. Knowing your own limitations is far better than overestimating other people, because you soon realize that everyone else has the same limitations. No one can stop you but you. You are as in control as anybody else. You have the added plus of knowing the only real "secret" to wealth: what you pay is the *only* thing you fully control. This "secret," though simple, is huge.

Chapter Three Takeaways

- A 401(k) or 403(b) is a company sponsored retirement plan. It is the surest way to wealth for a working person.

- 401(k)s usually invest in mutual funds, pools of money used to buy financial instruments.

- Stocks represent shares of ownership in companies. They have historically been the best way to grow wealth.

- Companies (and stocks) come in all shapes and sizes.

- Growth and value investing are the two major investing styles.

- REITs are real estate investment trusts

- Don't ignore opportunities abroad!

- Cash has a big hidden danger!

- Bonds are debt issued by companies or government entities.

- Bonds normally stabilize a portfolio.

- Dollar cost averaging is the most reliable way to "buy low, sell high."

- Pay attention to costs! It's the *only* thing you actually control.

IV

The Best Path To Financial Independence For The Working Person

Though *that* you execute is far more important than *how* you execute once you've made up your mind to grab the prosperity that is within your reach, my preferred method is to start at the end and to work backwards from there. In somewhat less flowery terms: I think saving for retirement is more important than paying-off every penny you owe as quickly as possible or starting an emergency fund. I came to this conclusion on a hot summer's day in 1989. Ironically, I had never seriously thought about money before this particular day except in the vaguest terms. I was going to be rich one day; that was just a simple fact of life. I would most likely get there via rock stardom. If that didn't work out, I would knock Stephen King off his perch as the premier writer of horror novels in the world. Barring those two things, I would win the lottery. I was probably going to win the lottery anyway. I bought a ticket every Thursday night back in those days; the law of averages was bound to catch up with me sooner or later. What I never even considered was that a guy who drove a truck could make a very nice life for himself on just a truck driver's wage.

My boss, Al, informed me that I would be working mandatory overtime on Saturday to make up for Wednesday when I wouldn't be going out on the road. I was required to go to a meeting on Wednesday about this new thing the company was starting called a 401(k). I was furious. I didn't mind overtime during the week, but the idea of driving to New York and Connecticut on a Saturday bummed me out beyond belief. I protested. I didn't need no stinkin'

401(k). Al, as usual, was utterly indifferent to my complaints. For not the first time he reminded me that if I didn't like something I was free to quit at any time. I grumbled to my colleague in the warehouse, Keith. Keith didn't mind going to this meeting because for him it was just a way of getting out of work for an hour. He wasn't the one being required to work on Saturday. I resigned. I resigned myself to the fact that I would have to go to this stupid meeting.

Keith and I walked across the freight yard to the offices that Wednesday morning. I was still in a foul mood. This was exacerbated by the fact we were in the midst of a boiling heat wave. The conference room was packed. Keith and I duly took seats in the back near the other guys wearing work boots, ratty jeans, and T-shirts, as far away from the office "suits" as we could get.

After a few minutes, a man and a woman walked into the room. The woman was breathtakingly beautiful, which turned out to be life-changing for me. It was life-changing because I hung on her every word and paid far closer attention than I might have otherwise. They were from Fidelity Investments.

It was at this meeting where I first learned what stocks and mutual funds were. Although I had heard of these things before, no one had ever really explained them to me and I had never been curious enough to ask. The man and the woman took turns with the pointer. They were both very good teachers. None of my high school math teachers had ever made graphs even slightly interesting, let alone fascinating. They explained compounding. Though I had once heard that the $24 worth of trinkets the Dutch had "bought" Manhattan for would have compounded to trillions of dollars by now, the fact that I could potentially be a millionaire someday just by working at this dump was something I could really appreciate. They explained the correlation between owning companies and wealth in simple terms I could understand. I didn't need to go into business for myself to own a company; I could own big name companies just by buying their stock. This appealed to me immensely. I couldn't go to Kmart and help myself to free stuff, but I could walk around the store with the knowledge that I owned the place.

Perhaps it was just a coincidence, or maybe a twist of fate, but I saw something that changed my life forever as Keith and I were leaving the meeting. One of the office clerks had a retirement statement sitting in front of him. I peeked at it as surreptitiously as I could. He had $100,000! The guy was no spring chicken, but he also wasn't a big money guy either. He was a clerk who filed blueprints for a living. It was true, then. An average person could amass a fortune. This guy who I knew for a fact wasn't making much more than I could with overtime had done it. I was flabbergasted. A hundred thousand dollars was a lot of money in 1989.

"I'm not doing it," Keith said as we walked out into the blazing sun. "I want my money now."

He was unpersuaded (or maybe just didn't believe me when I told him about the clerk).

"You could be a rich man, even working in this hole," I said.

"Yeah. I could be a rich man when I'm 59 ½," he said dismissively. "I might not even live that long. Even if I do, what good's money when you're 59 ½? You're old and washed-up by then. Go ahead and sign-up. *You'll* have plenty of money to give to the doctor and the undertaker. *I'd* rather live now."

I enrolled later that day. In retrospect, it was the smartest thing I ever did.

The keys to successful retirement investing are to start as early in life as you can, contribute the maximum amount you can afford to, pick age-appropriate investments, and to re-balance your portfolio every year.

Starting early is (or should be) self-evident. Time is a huge factor in growing wealth. Even modest amounts saved early enough will snowball into a large nest egg through the sheer force of time alone. Albert Einstein is said to have called compound interest "the most powerful force in the universe." (Sorry, he almost certainly didn't say it, but why let a good urban legend go to waste?) Compound interest is, nevertheless, one of those enormously powerful potentialities in the world that surrounds us, but that few people really consider and even fewer fully harness to their benefit. Compounding is a good example of the butterfly effect. The butterfly effect is when seemingly small things (such as a butterfly flapping its wings in Mexico) have dramatic consequences (such as cyclones in the Indian Ocean as a result of the tiny air disturbances caused by the butterfly in Mexico years earlier). The point is, slow and steady can seem as boring as hell when you're going through the daily grind, but the results–especially after you've been doing it for awhile–can be dramatic. The day eventually comes where your year-end dividends are more than your annual contributions!

Time is a great equalizer. We all get our allotment, and that's it. Rich people may have the money to eat better and to pay for better healthcare, but we all (with many tragic exceptions) get our 75 odd years and not much more. If more time could be bought, rich people would be buying it in droves.

To illustrate how time can be an equalizer, let's consider the case of the high school graduate versus the college graduate. With the caveat that I am *always* in favor of higher education if a person is cut out for it, let's suppose that a guy graduates high school and lands a pretty good job that enables him to contribute $100 a week to a 401(k) while another guy goes to a decent state university. Let's suppose the college student will graduate debt-free after four years (an increasingly rare scenario), but will contribute nothing to a retirement plan while he is in school. He will, however, be able to contribute $200 a week to a 401(k) once he graduates college because he will be earning considerably more than the high school graduate. At age 65, both men will be millionaires assuming a six percent return on their money throughout their working lives. The high school graduate will have $1,235,703.14; the college graduate will have $1,950,063.80. If the high school graduate had waited until age 22 to start contributing his $5,200 a year, he would have $975,031.90. Not a millionaire, but not half bad either. Both these men end up with a very healthy nest egg, but recall the high school graduate contributed only little more than *half* as much money as the college graduate. Such is the power of time.

Like my old buddy Keith, a lot of younger people put a low priority on retirement saving. They want to live *now*. Thirty, let alone 40, 50, or 60, is an eternity away. The old-timers at my first real job out of high school used to have a mantra that they would drill into my head at every opportunity. "Pay yourself first," they would say. This meant that the money I owed myself was at least as important as the bill I paid to my car insurance company. It took a few years and a 401(k) enrollment meeting for me to finally start listening to them, but I can see now what they meant. I didn't have to live like Ebenezer Scrooge to do alright in life. Paying myself first was just another bill that I would soon get used to paying. In fact, if I did it right from the start, I would never even miss the money. There is a very loose rule of thumb in the investing world that if you save 10% of your pay from the very start of your working life, you will be okay. If you save 15%, you will be affluent. If you save 20%, you will be very rich. For people like my old pal Keith who envision retirement saving as the thing that prevents all possible fun for an entire working lifetime and getting older as something so far away that it's not worth thinking about now, Einstein *did* have an applicable quote. "I never worry about the future; it comes soon enough."

If there is one glaring difference between the rich and everyone else, it's that rich people own stocks. Fully 50% of American households do not own even a single share in an individual stock or a stock mutual fund. Simple fear is a major reason for this. Stocks are mysterious things to those only glancingly familiar with them, things seemingly laden with potential danger. This perception is both a shame and tremendously costly. Stocks are the only other vehicle besides rolling the dice on one's own business or higher education available to the vast majority of poor, working-, and middle class people by which one might climb the economic ladder.

Asset allocation is simply how you divide your 401(k) contributions amongst stocks, bonds, and cash. With the full understanding that many people will put all their money into Guaranteed Investment Contracts at the start because cash is seemingly safe, there will come a time when you need to plunge into the stock and bond markets. Fortune favors the bold.

Everyone needs stocks. They are wealth-building engines. Some people, however, should have more stocks than others. The goal of successful asset allocation is to construct an age-appropriate portfolio. Younger people can afford to load-up their portfolios with stocks because they have the luxury of time which smooths-out market volatility. Older workers, on the other hand, need a larger percentage of their money in "safe" investments like bonds and cash to avoid the possibility of losing a large portion of their money right on the eve of retirement as happened to many people during the Great Recession. Older workers do, nonetheless, need to keep *some* money in stocks. Where in the old days retirements usually consisted of two or three years spent rocking in a rocking chair before death, now retirements routinely last 20 or 30 years. That's a lot of time for inflation to gobble-up purchasing power. Running out of money in retirement is a far greater risk than dying with too much money.

Asset allocation is far more art than science. The old conventional wisdom among financial advisors was that you should have 100 minus your age in stocks (as a percentage), and the rest in bonds. For those with a high risk tolerance,

120 minus your age in stocks was the general rule. This advice doesn't seem bad to me, but some people will be overcautious and others absolute daredevils. Asset allocation is a very personal decision. If you are the least bit unsure about what to do, it doesn't hurt to take advantage of the free financial advice many companies now offer to their retirement plan participants through the plan administrator.

If the goal of asset allocation is to make your portfolio age-appropriate, it will naturally need to be re-balanced as you get older. This is one of the trickiest parts of investing, one that our human tendency towards inertia makes even tougher. If you follow the 100 minus your age rule, you will need to realign your portfolio every year. If the stock market has a banner year while your bonds go nowhere (or vice versa) your portfolio will be out of whack. To re-balance, you will need to sell some of your winners and buy more of your losers. This sounds counterintuitive, but remember, the key to financial success is to buy low and sell high. This is exactly what you're doing when you re-balance.

What if all this sounds too daunting? What if you have no confidence in your ability to wisely allocate your assets and no desire whatsoever to tweak your portfolio every New Year's Day?

You're in luck.

"Life-cycle" or "target date" funds are a relatively new financial product that takes full advantage of the human propensities towards fear, inertia, and vacillation, but all to the investor's favor. With names like "Retirement 2020," "Retirement 2030," or "Financial Freedom 2050" target date funds are "funds of funds," that is, prepackaged mutual funds made up of other mutual funds that provide an instant ready-made portfolio based on the investor's current age. Containing the appropriate mix of stocks, bonds, and cash, all the investor needs to do is pick the year that most closely matches the year in which he or she wishes to retire. The real beauty of target date funds for the only casually interested (or nervous) investor is that re-balancing is done automatically. As the investor ages, the proportion of stocks to bonds and cash falls. Target date funds are truly a way to "set it and forget it" for those who prefer to put their retirement saving on autopilot.

While I think target date funds are a fabulous invention for those who would otherwise invest inappropriately, they are not perfect. My major problem with them is that most do not contain nearly enough foreign stocks. Much, if not most, stock gains will come from abroad in the coming decades in my opinion. Though it's true that the multinationals these funds contain will benefit from this trend, I think the real danger to younger investors will be in missing out rather than the risks inherent in international investing.

So far I have mentioned 401(k)s numerous times throughout this book, but what if your company has a lousy 401(k), or worse, offers no 401(k) at all?

The Individual Retirement Account, a.k.a. the IRA, is a retirement plan administered by you instead of a company. You (or your spouse in the case of a "spousal" IRA) must fund this investment from money you actually earn. An IRA cannot be funded with "unearned" income, such as a gift from your parents or lottery winnings. If you make a lot of money and are covered by a plan at work such as a 401(k) or 403(b), you can still contribute to an IRA, but there is a cutoff after which the tax deductibility of your contributions is phased-out. The other chief drawbacks to an IRA in contrast to a 401(k) are as follows: signing up for an IRA requires you to be proactive. IRAs do not come with a company match. IRAs do not offer the same legal protections as company retirement plans in some states, and contribution limits are far lower than what you can legally contribute to a 401(k) or 403(b). Other than that, IRAs are all upside.

IRAs offer nearly unlimited choice to the active investor, and a plethora of great choices for those who would prefer not to think about it. Unlike the 401(k) investor, you are not limited to just a few choices from a small menu of investment offerings. IRA investors can buy into literally thousands of different mutual funds, individual stocks, REITs, and even silver and gold. All manner of target date funds are, of course, available, as are super cheap index funds. Emerging market stocks and bonds and even frontier market mutual funds, rarely offered in 401(k)s, are freely available to the IRA investor. Many hands-on investors prefer IRAs to 401(k)s for the choices alone.

There are two types of IRA: the Traditional IRA and the Roth.

Traditional IRAs work very much like 401(k)s. Contributions are tax-deferred until the money is withdrawn, preferably in retirement. This means that you will not pay taxes on the money you contribute until years later (when you will be taxed at whatever your ordinary tax rate is then). If you make $35,000 a year and contribute $5,000 to your IRA, you will only pay taxes on $30,000. Tax deferral is huge because *all* of your money will be working for you.

Unlike 401(k)s which have contribution limits of $17,500 a year as of 2014 ($23,000 for people over age 50), IRAs, both Traditional and Roth, have limits of $5,500 for people under 50 (and $6,500 for people over 50). These limits are not a problem for most working people. I know very few people able to save $17,500 a year for retirement. The phase-out numbers (the point where a Traditional IRA is no longer fully tax deductible and beyond which it's not tax deductible at all for people with access to a company retirement plan) are $60,000 to $70,000 for single people and $96,000-$116,000 for married couples. The Roth phase-out numbers are $114,000-$129,000 for single people, and $181,000-$191,000 for married couples.

The Traditional IRA is a great option for those whose companies don't match 401(k) contributions, have lousy and/or expensive menu options, or don't offer a 401(k) in the first place. It's very easy to set up automatic deductions from your paycheck or bank account. The IRA business is very competitive; this means companies will be fighting for your business. That's always a good thing for the consumer.

Many people who do participate in company-sponsored retirement plans also fund an IRA on the side. This is most often because, although the company doesn't have the greatest fund choices, it offers a company match. Always, always, always take free money. Even if your company offers garbage in the way of investment options, always contribute up to the full company match. It's the only free lunch you'll ever get in this world.

The Roth IRA (along with the still not yet common Roth 401(k)) is simply the greatest thing since sliced bread. Named for the former Delaware senator William Roth who wrote the bill that became the law that bears his name, the Roth IRA is a potential wealth factory. The reason for this is that it is not, unlike a 401(k), 403(b), or Traditional IRA tax-advantaged. It's *tax-free*.

Where the other retirement vehicles are tax-deferred, meaning you get a tax break each week (thus a $100 weekly deduction won't reduce your take-home pay by $100), the Roth IRA is not tax-deferred. You pay every penny in tax owed right away. The *earnings* on your investments are, however, tax-free. Forever. If the Roth IRA had been around in 1965 and you had bought 20 shares of Berkshire Hathaway at 18 bucks a share, you would today have more than $3,500,000. You would owe Uncle Sam exactly zilch on this money.

You could blow the IRS a kiss goodbye as you were pulling out of New York Harbor on your round-the-world luxury cruise.

One fear many Roth IRA participants have is that some future Congress, addicted to other people's money as nearly all politicians are, will find the tax-free Roth money irresistible and rewrite the law so they can grab some of it. This could happen, but we live in the here and now. It's best not to worry about something until there is something to worry about. Besides, if Congress ever backtracks on its promise and proposes a tax on Roth earnings, it's just as likely that people who have gotten rich from Roth IRAs will just band together, hire some lobbyists, and buy a whole new Congress!

The Roth IRA is another reason some 401(k) participants invest beyond their company plans. Though it has historically been a good idea to grab a tax break when you can get it (such as in a tax-deferred 401(k)), it's almost a certainty that tax rates will never again be as low as they are right now. Remember, you will be paying ordinary tax rates on your withdrawals in retirement. Those ordinary rates may well be much higher than the tax rates you're paying now. We are a nation with a serious debt problem, rotting infrastructure, and an aging population who have been made a lot of promises. A Roth IRA, either alone or in tandem with a retirement plan at work, is a good hedge against an uncertain future.

Saving for retirement is the best path to prosperity. Though my old friend Keith saw retirement saving as almost an admission of and concession to a mortality unworthy of acknowledgement, it really is not. Saving for retirement is just a protracted process with a destination that seems very vague in the beginning. Indeed, you might not ever get there. No man is promised tomorrow. The process, however, mirrors life in that it consists of long stretches of boredom punctuated by moments of joy, regret, and sheer terror. As mundane as the task can sometimes seem, saving for retirement is all about building a better life in an as yet unknowable future. It is, of all things, worth doing. The present you has an obligation to the future you. Many people, sadly, will find they have earned the contempt of their future selves merely because they never bothered to consider them in the present.

There is a thing called the "wealth effect." This is where people *feel* rich because the values of their homes or portfolios have gone up. Although they don't necessarily sell their homes or cash-out their stocks, these unrealized paper gains make them feel flush. Recall that most self-made people are not motivated by materialism; they crave security. The wealth effect is really just an intangible feeling of well-being. Some people spend money as a result of the wealth effect. They might take that trip to Paris or buy that new car. They may even borrow money to do it. There is nothing wrong with this. Most financial advisors would wag their fingers at such profligacy, as if borrowing money for such frivolities was the crime of the century, but I disagree. Life is to be enjoyed, as long as it is enjoyed in moderation. I certainly wouldn't use retirement savings for a vacation, but I have put vacations on credit cards with the knowledge that I could always cash-out some investments if I couldn't pay the bill any other way. I here and now confess to that most awful of financial sins: I myself have carried a credit card balance for a trip to Paris.

It's very hard for many people, young people especially, to wrap their minds around the fact that money saved for retirement is not gone money. There is very little difference between 60 years old and 90 when you're 18. Ironically, most teenagers think they'll live forever yet somehow never get old. This is a peculiarity of the adolescent brain that is almost universal. When given a choice between future prosperity or a fun night out on the town, younger people will most often choose the latter. The major reason people delay saving for retirement is that money put into a 401(k) or IRA seems to many like money thrown away into the black hole of future time.

Money in an IRA or 401(k) is not, in fact, gone money. You can always take your money out. It's a terrible idea. You will pay tax immediately, as well as a stiff penalty if you are under 59 ½, but it can be done. Most 401(k)s come with a borrowing option. You can borrow half of the balance up to $50,000 in most cases. The interest on these loans is paid to yourself. Except under the direst circumstances, 401(k) loans are also a bad idea. Though paying interest to yourself sounds great, lost compounding generally makes a 401(k) loan a losing proposition. In the event you quit your job or get fired, the entire loan balance will be due within 60 days. If you cannot pay, you will be considered in default and owe taxes and most likely a penalty.

Although it is possible to access your retirement savings before retirement age (and almost always a horrible decision to actually do so), there are a myriad of benefits to not doing it. Aside from the obvious fact that you are securing your golden years, there is the wealth effect. This is the peace of mind of just knowing the money is there. Once you reach a certain balance (usually well before retirement age), you realize that you could survive for *years* if you were suddenly let go from your job and unable to find another. The day to day worries of the paycheck to paycheck life become things you *used* to worry about. Deep in your heart you know that you could always take out a 401(k) loan to buy a new car if you absolutely had to. Then, there are the incremental victories. Crossing the $100,000 threshold is like nothing else to a working- or middle class person. That's *a lot* of money. Looking at the first year-end statement in which you made $12,000 in dividends and/or capital gains can take your breath away. That's $1,000 a month just for owning companies (minus the headaches small business owners endure). You start to really understand the expression "it takes money to make money" at this point. Your money is the thing that is making you all this money.

Rich people get special perks unavailable to everyone else. One of these perks is special treatment by financial firms to those with large account balances. While I would usually advocate leaving an old 401(k) from a previous job where it is or rolling it over into the 401(k) at your new job, some people opt to roll their old retirement plans into an IRA. This process is often a formerly working- or middle class person's first glimpse into the rarified air of the affluent life. Firms will fight furiously for your business if you're rolling over six figures. If you are rolling over enough money, you will get things such as a dedicated customer service person (which means you will *never* be put on hold or kept waiting), free subscriptions, free consultations with financial advisors who might charge other clients thousands of dollars for a comprehensive financial plan, no junk fees of any kind, lower expense ratios, and commission-free brokerage trades. It's good to be the king.

Though retirement saving is not the only vehicle that can carry you on the long road to prosperity it is, in my opinion, the best one.

Chapter Four Takeaways

- Company-sponsored retirement plans such as 401(k)s give the common person immediate access to the tools wealthy people use to get that way.

- You can finance almost anything, but you can't finance retirement.

- Start as early as you can and save as much as you can to take maximum advantage of compounding.

- Investments need to be age-appropriate.

- A portfolio should be re-balanced every year.

- Pay yourself first!

- Target date funds make investing simple.

- IRAs are self-directed retirement plans.

- Roth IRAs grow tax-free!

- If your company offers a 401(k) match, take it. Never turn down free money!

V

The Emergency Fund

Ideally, the emergency fund is for emergencies. This might seem an obvious statement of fact, but you would be surprised at what some people consider "emergencies." Bad brakes on your car is an emergency, an acquaintance's destination wedding on the beach in Jamaica is not. A broken furnace in January or a burst water pipe is definitely an emergency. A sale at your favorite department store is not an emergency. A screaming toothache is an emergency; that your buddy has an extra ticket to an NFL playoff game because the guy who was originally going to go suddenly needs a root canal is not an emergency. A leaky roof is an emergency. A big sale at . . . Well, you get the idea.

Whether you start on the path to financial independence by starting an emergency fund or some other way, everyone should *eventually* have an emergency fund. An adequate emergency fund contains at least three to six months' living expenses in a liquid account. In the wake of the Great Recession, some financial advisors recommend that you save an entire *years'* pay. This is not realistic for most working people (and probably not necessary if you are saving in a 401(k)). In fact, saving three to six months' salary is no easy feat. Still, that should be the ultimate goal.

Like investing for retirement or attacking a large credit card debt, building an emergency fund is an incremental process. The temptation for some people is to throw every cent they can into a savings account as quickly as possible in order to achieve their three to six months' target, but this is a risky strategy for many. Especially if they are living on a diet of cold oatmeal and shivering under blankets in freezing weather just to wring-out a few extra bucks for their savings account. Saving too much too fast can easily cause burnout. The problem with specific goals such as saving a set amount of money within a self-imposed time limit is that, if things don't go exactly as planned, frustration sets in. This frustration can easily be the thing that causes us to throw up our hands and give up on the whole enterprise. It is not at all uncommon for an emergency to happen while an emergency fund is under construction. It takes a certain mental toughness to get back up and dust yourself off once you have been knocked down by such a setback. Emergency funds are easily given up on. That's why I recommend that they be funded on a regular basis with a *very* modest sum of money. So what if it takes a long time to reach your goal? As long as you are making forward progress (and learn to deal with the very setbacks emergency funds exist for in the first place) there is no set dollar figure you need to achieve in order to feel that you have "won" the game.

Temptation is a huge problem for savers in highly liquid savings vehicles. The very fact that the money is easy to get at is, in and of itself, the problem for a lot of people. When I was a little kid and my grandfather would give me a few bucks, he would always say: "Don't let that money burn a hole in your pocket." I didn't know what he was talking about the first several times he said this, but eventually figured it out. If I quit blowing all my money on junk, I could eventually save up for something I really wanted. Though I didn't become a good saver until many years later, the seed was planted.

Building an emergency fund takes self-discipline, but for me anyway, the further I got in the process the easier the process got. Momentum can be a huge motivator. While some people will inevitably fail as soon as they reach the thousand dollar mark (by celebrating the fact they've saved a thousand bucks by treating themselves to something that costs a thousand bucks), many people will see this as just the first milestone on the road that potentially leads to a million dollars.

There is a colossal psychological victory that the self-disciplined saver experiences very early in the game. When viewed as the achievement that it truly is, it can be literally life-altering. It takes only one weeks' pay saved to accomplish, but it often somehow changes everything. This is escaping the paycheck to paycheck quicksand that swallows millions and keeps millions more chained to a bad company, an evil boss, or a lifetime stuck in neutral.

A weeks' pay is not a lot of money to the vast majority of people, but the psychological implications of saving that amount can be immense. Suddenly, you're two paychecks away from catastrophe instead of one. Soon it will be three, then ten, then 26. Of course, you can't tell the boss what you really think of him or his two-bit company, but you have achieved financial independence, if only a weeks' worth. This is a harbinger of things to come and should be viewed that way. Suddenly, you are no longer completely beholden to a single company. You have, in a sense, earned 7 days of freedom. Soon it will be much, much more. This is the truest and purest financial freedom. This is what we strive for when we take those first wobbly baby steps toward financial independence.

The best way to start an emergency fund is to have a manageable amount of money automatically deducted from your paycheck or checking account and put into a savings account. By manageable I mean a sum that won't prevent you from paying your bills (including that most important one, your 401(k) contribution). If it's only five or ten bucks a week, that's still progress. Remember, in case of dire emergencies (and I do mean *dire*) you can borrow or withdraw money from your 401(k). If you have to carry a balance on your credit card to pay for a car repair so as not to kill yourself or other motorists, so be it. A big part of financial success is learning to deal with setbacks. If a true emergency happens and you have to find other financial means to deal with it, that's just the way it is. One of the reasons I advocate saving small and steady in an emergency fund is that frequently something will come up that you cannot afford to pay with funds from your savings account. You may have to pay the car mechanic $300 to fix your car, but have only $200 in the emergency fund. In this case I would put it on the credit card, pay it off as quickly as possible without stopping savings deposits, and grit my teeth that I was paying much more in interest than I was receiving. In the long run, a few bucks more paid in interest will certainly be more than offset by having kept your momentum alive.

Eventually you will reach your goal. It may take years, but if you are self-disciplined enough you will get there. What then?

Once you have saved three to six months' living expenses, the emergency fund is a great place to park additional money for the things you want. A life of unrelenting drudgery is not living at all. Way too many financial writers ignore the fact that real life doesn't always fit into the neat little template they have created that covers all the bases for accumulating money, but doesn't take into consideration that you might want to spend some of it someday.

You may want that trip to Hawaii, that new car, or that deck. Though these things may not make sense to the financial advisor whose brain is really just a sophisticated accounting machine with absolutely no provision for fun, life on Earth is finite. It should be enjoyed. While happiness can never be a permanent condition (even for the Warren Buffetts of the world) life has its moments. Money makes more of those moments possible. Whoever said money cannot buy happiness was more inaccurate than wrong. Money can't buy permanent happiness, but it sure can buy little bursts of it. The Beatles were absolutely wrong when they said that "fun is the one thing that money can't buy."

All that being said, it is far better to save for the things you want than to buy things on impulse. The key to doing this is to set a minimum balance for your emergency fund and to save on top of that balance for the things that will give you enjoyment. In the event an emergency happens you may have to put off that vacation until your balance is rebuilt, but once you have reached three to six months' living expenses, you've proven you're a pretty disciplined saver anyway. You know you will get to Hawaii sooner or later.

While I am a fan of the emergency fund, I am not a fan of emergency funds that are too big. A years' pay in a savings account seems unreasonable to me in a near-zero interest rate environment. After taxes, savings account interest rates don't even match, let alone beat, inflation. Still, savings accounts are a great way to save for short-term goals. Any money earmarked for longer-term plans, however, should be somewhere else. Your infant's college savings, for instance, should not be in a savings account.

There are a few (and I've met some of them) people out there to whom accumulating money *is* their fun. One of these people actually used his savings account as a springboard to build his fortune. He would save a few thousand dollars beyond his emergency fund, then, after thinking it over for a short while, buy an investment of some kind or other. It might be a plain-vanilla index mutual fund, an emerging markets fund, an individual stock, or a gold coin. All were more or less impulse buys; too much planning would have taken the fun and spontaneity out of it. There are certainly better ways to invest (such as retirement savings, which he did as well), but the "extra" money in his emergency fund was his play money. He did very well. It's not that he was an expert stock picker or made better choices than everyone else; he just built an extremely diversified investment portfolio while having his idea of fun at the same time. Ironically, he was always making money in something no matter what the economy was doing.

Many ordinary people have used the emergency fund as their starting point to affluence. In the old days, when traditional pensions were the norm, Wall Street was an arcane world to all but the very rich. Everybody knew things went on there, but few understood exactly what. These things were the concern of the people your company paid to administer the pension fund, not yours. In the event a person was to make the leap from the middle class to the upper class, he or she would find people who could navigate this world. Usually, this was a brokerage house. Unlike today where you can research a stock online then, with the click of a mouse, buy shares for next to nothing in commissions, brokerage houses back then were "full service." They would do all the research, recommend the stocks you should buy, execute trades on floors full of screaming people waving papers around, and either hold your stock certificates or send them to you. All this cost a lot of money. The new investor typically got this money by scrimping and saving for years, most often in a run-of-the-mill savings account.

Sadly, the middle class was much richer then, even as it was much more difficult (from a technical perspective) to climb to the next rung on the economic ladder than it is today. Well-paying jobs were plentiful, there was a chicken in every pot, and a house with a white picket fence was the aspiration of most. The icing on the cake was a little nest egg, most often held in a bland savings account or certificates of deposit. The real reason people were richer, however, is that, unlike today, the vast majority had lived through the Great Depression and World War II and understood the now rapidly fading concept of "enough."

Saving money in an emergency fund is not easy, but for those with the self-discipline, it's a great way to get started on the path to financial independence. There will be setbacks. Everybody gets a flat tire sooner or later. There will definitely be temptations. A big part of financial success is just not shooting yourself in the foot. Despite these minor downsides, the rewards are quick and large. Escaping paycheck to paycheck purgatory is like releasing a helium balloon. The paycheck to paycheck life can always jump up and grab you once you are first released, but at some point you will fly away.

If you do decide that starting your emergency fund is your preferred means of execution, my advice to you is the same advice my grandfather gave to me.

Don't let that money burn a hole in your pocket!

Chapter Five Takeaways

- Everyone should *eventually* have an emergency fund.

- Emergency funds are for *emergencies*.

- Any excess saved beyond your target should be used to buy something you want or invested.

VI

Credit: A Double-Edged Sword

Rich people have "leverage." Everybody else has "credit." The ultimate goal for the person who aspires to financial independence should be to parlay his or her credit into leverage. The chief difference between leverage and credit is that leverage gives advantage while credit, very frequently, puts the user of it at a profound disadvantage. What are these advantages of leverage? Perhaps the best one is the ability to arbitrage. Nothing illustrates the chasm between the rich and everyone else like arbitrage. Arbitrage, in a nutshell, is the fine art of getting something for nothing. While I previously wrote that a company 401(k) match is the only thing you'll ever get for free, I was mistaken. I forgot to mention arbitrage. A great example of arbitrage is this: Japan in the 1990s, already well into an economic malaise that would last for decades, had lending rates near zero. American banks, at the time, were still paying decent interest rates on deposits. Shrewd arbitragers (who naturally had leverage) realized they could borrow money from Japanese banks, deposit these millions or billions into American bank accounts, pay the Japanese loans down with the interest they were being paid by American banks, and pocket the very substantial difference. Whatever one thinks about the ethics of this, few would argue that it wasn't brilliant.

Unfortunately, most of us can't use leverage like this. Japanese banks are not likely to lend Joe or Jane Sixpack money, even if he or she has a credit score over 800. The one way in which an average person *can* use leverage, however, is by getting the best possible terms on any loan and making lenders compete for your business. The way to do this is by having the highest possible credit score.

The credit score is an arcane, mysterious thing. *Exactly* how it's calculated is one of those questions similar to what happened to all those ships and planes that vanished in the Bermuda Triangle or whether Lee Harvey Oswald really acted alone, a question that will probably never be answered to everyone's satisfaction.

All joking aside, the credit score *is* a seemingly capricious thing. Developed by Fair Isaac Corporation, the credit (or FICO) score is a number between 300-850 that impacts your life *dramatically* whether you realize it or not. This number determines if you get a loan, what interest rate you will pay if you do get it, whether or not you can rent an apartment, and even whether or not you get a job. All manner of data go into calculating a credit score. How long you have had credit, your payment history, how much credit you have available, and your debt to income ratio will all heavily influence your credit score. Even *checking* your credit too often can ding your credit score! The average credit score in America is anywhere between 661-711 depending on which source you believe. That's not too good. Anything under 640 is considered "subprime," while a score of at least 740 (preferably 750 or higher) is necessary to get the most favorable rates on loans. Curiously, I have never met (or even heard of) anyone with a credit score of 850. It's possible such a person exists, but then again, the Loch Ness Monster, Bigfoot, or the Abominable Snowman might really exist too.

As in so many other facets of personal finance, you can only control what you can control. The key to a good credit rating is to pay all your bills on time, month in and month out. While you can improve your credit score by doing such things as limiting your available credit (by asking your credit card issuer to reduce your available credit) and not applying for new credit too frequently, paying your bills consistently will, more than anything else, improve or maintain your credit score.

Just a quick note on credit scores: your Fico score is the only one that matters. Some credit bureaus (those companies that collect your data from lenders) have jumped on the credit score/identity theft protection bandwagon in recent years. One of these companies actually invented its own credit score with its own numbers that do not correlate to the Fico score. Go with Fico. You can bet your lenders will!

As mentioned in chapter one, knowing where you stand is a good starting point. In the realm of credit, checking your credit should be the first step.

Every American is entitled to one free credit report each year from each of the three major credit bureaus (Experian, TransUnion, and Equifax). These reports can be accessed by going to annualcreditreport.com. Checking your free reports will not have a negative effect on your credit score. You will not get your credit score from these reports, but you will get enough information for you to make an educated ballpark guess as to what it might be. (If you want to know your actual credit score you can buy it directly from Fair Isaac for a nominal fee by going to myfico.com.)

It's extremely important that your credit reports be accurate; alas, many aren't. If you find any inaccuracies in your credit reports, dispute them immediately with the credit bureau *in writing*. You can't fix negative information that is correct, such as a late payment three years ago, but you are absolutely entitled to demand that inaccurate information be removed. It is vitally important that you never pay a penny you don't owe. Some people think resolving a small debt will look better to a lender checking their report even if it's not really their debt. If the debt is not yours, DON'T PAY IT! Paying any portion of a debt is an acknowledgement that the debt is, in fact, yours and is red meat to collection agencies.

If your credit report does contain blemishes that are a result of tough times you may have had years ago, the only thing that can fix them is time. There are some very slimy "entities" (I will not give them the undeserved dignity of calling them "companies") out there who promise, for a fee, to "repair" your credit. Some people, hoping to qualify for a mortgage or a car loan, will turn to these "credit repair" agencies in the hopes that their mistakes of the past will be stricken from the official record. They won't be, at least not legally. The worst of these "companies" will commit fraud to "repair" the client's credit; the rest will just do nothing except take your money. There is nothing they can do you can't do yourself. The *only* way to repair your credit is to let time heal the wounds.

Negative information must be removed from your credit reports after seven years, with the exception of bankruptcies which stay on your credit report for 10 years. The good news is that a person diligently trying to improve his or her credit will not have to wait an entire seven years for a second chance. Two years' solid payment history is usually all it takes to get those pre-approved credit card offers to start pouring in. They won't be great deals (or even good deals), but will be tangible proof that your credit is in the process of healing.

Even people who have a bankruptcy in the their past can start the process of healing the damage long before 10 years have gone by. Bankruptcy used to contain a strong stigma. People who, knowing they are going to declare bankruptcy in the near future and therefore max-out their remaining credit cards, are indeed of questionable character. It's important to point out, however, that the *majority* of bankruptcies in recent years have been directly related to medical expenses. Having had to pay thousands of dollars out of pocket two years ago for a minor operation *despite* having insurance, I am much more inclined to blame the system than its victims. It's a national disgrace that we are the only civilized country in the world where you can be severely punished for the "crime" of getting sick.

If you have had credit problems in the past, forget about them. It's water under the bridge, spilt milk. The past, as they say, is a foreign country and tomorrow a brand new day. The best course for the future is to avoid debt as much as possible and to pay all your bills on time each month going forward.

Choosing the route of paying-off debt as a means to eventual financial freedom is generally a very smart choice. As I wrote earlier, with historic stock market returns averaging 9.4% and average credit card interest rates exceeding 13%, this choice seems a no-brainer. Especially since paying-off a debt charging 13% interest is essentially the same as *earning* 13%. That this 13% is tax-free is just an amazing cherry on top. Still, there are a few things to consider.

My chief argument against throwing every penny you've got at consumer debt is that you cannot finance retirement. Some people (to their credit) manage to retire enormous credit card debts, but it usually takes years. This is valuable time in which money could have been compounding, time lost forever. While I believe paying debts one has agreed to pay is a moral imperative, so too is not becoming a ward of the state because of a complete failure to plan for the future. The best approach to this conundrum, in my opinion, is to balance paying debts with retirement saving. It will take longer to pay-off the debts. It will certainly cost more in interest payments. You will not, however, end up debt-free but penniless. Though paying debts off is a laudable and worthy goal, having nothing but owing nothing still equals broke.

Another problem faced by those who choose to attack debt as a means to eventual affluence is the same one faced by those who go the emergency fund route. That is, money burning a hole in one's pocket. Unlike the saver who sees growth and knows progress is being made, however slowly, it is hard for many people to see a shrinking debt in the same light. Even for those who can, there is often a trap. This is to see the trees that are the minimum monthly payment instead of the forest that is the total debt. Some will undoubtedly redouble their efforts once the minimum monthly payments become smaller. They will continue to hammer away. Others, however, will reason that, since they could handle the old payment, it wouldn't hurt to treat themselves to something. After all, they've worked hard to get the monthly minimum down. Too often this results in the debt actually creeping *higher*.

An additional problem for these folks, one also faced by emergency fund savers, is the problem of setbacks. A person may have diligently paid down his or her debts for months, when the car suddenly breaks down. The bill might erase *all* of the progress made over months in a single day. Some will be able to pick themselves up, dust themselves off, and continue steady-on. Many others, however, won't. Utterly discouraged, many of these people will charge even *more* to assuage their disappointment through shopping. The real pity here is that the enterprise, with very few exceptions, is over at this point. This person might well conclude that the paycheck to paycheck life is as truly inescapable as they've heard or imagined, and just give up.

For those who do choose the debt elimination track, it's valuable to recall that rich people both use leverage and buy appreciating assets. In fact, rich people often use leverage *to* buy their appreciating assets.

Though some financial pundits see *any* kind of debt as absolutely toxic, most financial advisors classify debt as either "good debt" or "bad debt." Good debt is used to buy things that appreciate in value. A college education will presumably yield a better return that it costs. Houses have historically gone up in price faster than inflation. Student loans (though many people would now forcefully disagree) and mortgages (with an equal number of vociferous detractors) are "good" debts. Car loans, payday loans (God forbid!), and credit cards are "bad" debts. What this means is that not all debts are equal. Some should be attacked with a vengeance and others (primarily mortgage debt) not be paid-down at all beyond the required monthly payment.

One rule of thumb for deciding if it's worth it to pay down a debt faster than required is whether or not you could get a better return somewhere else.

Credit card debt is truly a no-brainer. You will not get a guaranteed 13% tax-free return anywhere. (If I am wrong and you do know of such an investment, please contact me immediately!) Car loans are less clear cut. People with stellar credit have been able to finance cars at ridiculously low rates in recent years. It doesn't make financial sense to pay ahead on a two percent auto loan when you could possibly earn 9.4% in a 401(k) with a tax advantage to boot. Similarly, paying extra on a mortgage is often not the best move. Although there is something to be said for owning your home outright, you can't eat home equity. A mortgage should never be paid ahead at the expense of retirement saving. Also, interest on mortgages is usually tax-deductible for those who itemize their taxes. This can add-up to a couple percentage points when calculating your true investment return. For people with stellar credit who have gotten mortgages under four percent in the past few years, the real rates are more like two percent when you factor-in the tax breaks!

After years of steady payments and good credit management, regular people finally get leverage. It's not the leverage enjoyed by the superrich. You almost certainly won't be able to borrow large amounts from foreign banks and invest the money in surefire investments, but it's leverage all the same. Once your credit score tops 800 it becomes not a matter of you being lucky enough to be approved for a loan, but the bank being lucky enough to get your business. A high credit score adds an additional layer of security to a person's life. Security, remember, is the real motive of most self-made investors. If wealthy people enjoy advantages in this world (which they do), not all of those advantages are unfair. A high credit score does not come overnight. It must be earned. Very few wealthy people have anything but stellar credit ratings. Some would argue that this is because they are rich and thus don't get knocked off their feet by something as mundane as needing new tires to pass inspection. This is only partially true. Wealthy people understand the gravity of their creditworthiness. Although many working- and middle class people fully understand just how bad bad credit can be, many don't really think about it until they are turned down for a mortgage or a car loan. Oftentimes the people who get into trouble with credit are young. They don't fully understand the ramifications of not paying a credit card bill on time, or get in over their heads because they are trying to impress their peers with some material object they've bought. While I truly have sympathy for those who get sick, lose their jobs unexpectedly, or fall on hard times as a result of circumstances beyond their control, I have met too many people who rail against banks when it is *they* who have no self-control. This stuff is serious, serious business. Fair or not, your creditworthiness is a direct reflection of your reputation.

If arbitrage can loosely be defined as the ability to get something for nothing, it just so happens that those who have nurtured and built their credit scores get to enjoy the fruits of arbitrage too! Frequently, automakers will offer zero percent financing to "well-qualified" buyers. That's you! Being able to finance a 20 or 30 thousand dollar car for just the principal is a steal. In the event you had the 20 or 30 grand saved-up, you could put that money to work somewhere else as you made the (pure principal) payments on the car. Rewards credit cards are a form of arbitrage. As many of these cards charge no annual fees or interest if the balance is paid in full each month, it's possible to get a new tablet, a telescope, or a flight to Europe for absolutely nothing!

Your credit can be the thing that gets you turned down for the job or a free flight to London. Credit truly is a double-edged sword. It can hurt a person badly or be a very effective tool for those who learn to wield it properly. As an old-timer warned me when I got my first credit card, however, you need to "manage it, manage it, manage it!"

Chapter Six Takeaways

- Paying-off high interest debt is a great way to start on the path to prosperity, but it takes much more self-discipline than other methods.

- Paying-down debt should not come at the expense of saving for retirement.

- Only time can heal bad credit.

- Check your credit reports for free three times a year at annualcreditreport.com

- Check your credit score (for a small fee) at myfico.com

- Stellar credit gives you the best rates and rewards like free travel, cash-back, and free stuff!

VII

A House: To Buy or Not to Buy, That is the Question

Buying a house is the single largest investment most working- and middle class people ever make. Historically it hasn't been a bad bet, but, contrary to popular belief, it hasn't been the best bet either. If you recall the example of my grandfather in an earlier chapter, his $5,000 investment is worth roughly $250,000 today. Had he invested his money in the stock market at the average annual rate of return of 9.4% instead of buying a house, however, his $5,000 would have grown to $1,002,286.78 by now. Of course, he had to live somewhere, but that was the whole point. A house, in my opinion, is not an investment. A house is somewhere you live. You should enjoy it, feel secure in it, and build your memories in it. You should not view it as a retirement plan, or far worse, a giant ATM. That's exactly what many people did in the heady years leading up to the Great Recession, and why so many people have since soured on homeownership.

Homeownership is not the panacea almost everyone thought it was up until the housing market began its meltdown at the end of 2007, and is most definitely not for everyone. Buying a house requires a lot more cash up front than renting an apartment. Unlike in an apartment, a leaky faucet, a broken toilet, or a clogged drain is on you. There is no maintenance person to call, just a (very expensive) plumber. If you hate your neighbors and live in an apartment, all you have to do is move out when the lease is up. If Satan and his family move in next door and you own your home, you have to sell it, put up with it, or wait him out. Whichever the case, you will likely be putting up with him for quite awhile. If you suddenly find yourself out of a job, it's a lot easier to go to where the jobs are if you don't need to sell a house first. Cruelly, many of the places where home prices fell the farthest also experienced the worst unemployment at the height of the Great Recession. Many of these areas have still not recovered. Few would have guessed that North Dakota would be the place to go when all was said and done. Renters have mobility where homeowners don't necessarily have stability.

Nevertheless, homeownership is still the ultimate goal of millions. It is far more symbolic of the "American Dream" than a large retirement nest egg. The "house with the white picket fence" is still, to many minds, the thing that indicates that you have made it, that you have arrived. There is a huge psychological component to homeownership. My brother frequently tells me that he needs "to feel soil that I know is mine" beneath his feet. (Ironically, he lives in an apartment and rents-out the house he owns. It's a long story for another book . . .) It is precisely because of this psychological component that affluent people tend to own their homes by a large margin. Most wealthy people, as I have said numerous times throughout this book, crave security far more than they covet diamonds, Bugattis, or Rembrandts. To them, there is something profoundly insecure about the perceived transience of the renting life. To not *own* a home is to not *have* a home, or a permanent one anyway, to their way of thinking. Where some people love the idea of being a carefree drifter, going where the weather "suits their clothes" and waking-up in a new place every morning, the prospect terrifies the person who fears insecurity.

Owning or renting your home is all really a matter of preference. Owning is not inherently superior to owning, and vice versa. To buy or not to buy a house is one of those questions that could cause you to waste a lot of paper writing-down the pros and cons. From a strictly financial point of view, the swiftly changing conventional wisdom that buying *always* beats renting is simply wrong. Theoretically, a renter could end up with *a lot* more wealth than someone who buys their home. Of course, the operative word here is "theoretically." The overwhelming majority of renters do not "invest the difference." In comparison, the homeowner has no choice but to fund his or her investment. Unless the area is decaying, the homeowner will build wealth through rising home equity on inflation alone.

One huge advantage many homeowners enjoy (aside from the mortgage interest deduction which is really just a government subsidy) is the stability of the fixed-rate mortgage. Where rents rise regularly, once a contract for a mortgage has been signed, the payment will not change for 30 years (except for changes in taxes and insurance if they are escrowed by the mortgage company). This means that, as inflation raises the prices of everything else, your payment will become more affordable as time goes by. To illustrate this, let me use the example of a couple I know. In 1997 they bought a house for $115,000. At the time they were renting an apartment for $600 a month. Their mortgage payment (including escrow) was going to be $900 a month. They were very nervous. An extra $300 a month was a lot of money to come up with. Fast forward to 2014. The $115,000 house is now appraised at $221,000. Their old apartment recently rented for $1,200 a month. Their mortgage payment is now just over $1,000 a month. Pretty nifty.

It's vital to keep in mind that, however hard it might seem to get a mortgage when lenders are demanding a credit score of at least 740 or 750, it's much easier to get into a house than out of one. You should not settle for a house any more than you'd settle for a romantic partner. If you can't get the house you really want, wait. Real estate agents can be notoriously pushy. An agent may imply you're a fool if you don't buy this certain house right away. As with romantic partners, there are lots of other fish in the sea. It's far better to extend the lease on your apartment than to buy a house just for the sake of buying a house. A house, of all things, should be a place you actually want to be.

If you do decide that homeownership is the right choice for you, make sure you do your homework. Though buying a house may not be the biggest *investment* you ever make, it will almost certainly be the biggest *purchase* you ever make.

As cliché as the saying has become, real estate is all about location, location, location. It makes no sense whatsoever to buy a house a two hour commute each way to and from your job. Get to know the neighborhood you're thinking of buying into. Is there a junk car in the driveway of the house next door to the one you're thinking of buying? That guy obviously doesn't care about his own property value; why would he care about yours? If you have school-aged kids (or even if you don't), check out the quality of the schools. Great schools are a good selling point; lousy schools will make the property less desirable if you ever decide to sell. Check the crime statistics. Do you really want to live with the worry that heroin addicts are ransacking your house while you're out working for a living? Buying a house is a process that, like getting married, is both stressful and exciting at the same time.

It pays to line-up financing as early as possible. Though some banks will "pre-qualify" you for a mortgage, this is essentially meaningless. You want to be "pre-approved." Being pre-approved for a mortgage gives you negotiating power. A seller is apt to take a lower bid if he is worried the higher bidder may not get financing.

Learn about mortgages. There are many different kinds. There are adjustable rate mortgages with annual percentage rates that change after a few years. Usually, they start off low and get higher (potentially much higher). I don't know why anybody would choose an adjustable rate mortgage in an interest rate environment like the one we are in where interest rates have nowhere to go but up. Fixed-rate mortgages generally come in 15, 20, or 30 year terms. Although shorter-term mortgages come with lower rates, they also come with higher monthly payments. I would always opt for the 30 year. There is nothing to stop you from making additional principal payments. In fact, although it is certainly not my preferred way to invest, many people pay their homes off early.

You will be given something called an "amortization table" at settlement. This will break down exactly what portion of your payment is principal, and what portion goes to interest each and every month for 30 years. In the beginning of a mortgage, most of the payment will go to interest. A $1,000 a month payment may be $900 interest, $100 principal. By paying the next month's principal (say by adding $102 to this month's check to be applied to next month's principal) you can drastically cut the amount of interest you pay. (Interest on $102 amortized over 29 years 11 months really adds-up!) If you do this consistently (with the understanding that those principal payments will get larger every single month) you will have a 30 year mortgage paid-off in 15 years!

Never buy more house than you can afford. This may sound trite or like one of those statements that make you want to say "no %&*@, Sherlock," but the sheer misery of being "house poor" is impossible to understate.

Almost everyone underestimates the true cost of homeownership. Many a McMansion buyer has felt the sting of that first heating or cooling bill; many don't think of how much these behemoths cost to heat and cool when they're working out the numbers to see if they can afford the mortgage. A dying tree that overhangs the street is not only the homeowner's responsibility, but a task most people would be wise to leave to the professionals. Tree work, by the way, often runs into the thousands. Do you have a pit bull or a Rottweiler? In the event your insurance company will even cover "dangerous" breeds you may well pay a hefty rider for your pal. My town has a curious habit of making anyone selling a house replace the sidewalk before the new homeowner moves in. Masonry work is not cheap. To my mind, you should *live* in a house, not merely exist there. Owning a house should not mean that you can never go on vacation again or that your kids get a pair of socks (and *only* a pair of socks) for Christmas.

Any financial advisor worth his or her salt would advise that you have at least 20% of the purchase price to put down as a down payment. One big reason for this is PMI. PMI (private mortgage insurance) is an insurance policy that covers the lender in case the borrower defaults on the mortgage. This insurance doesn't benefit the borrower in the least, but he or she pays the premiums nonetheless. This insurance can potentially cost thousand of dollars a year! At 20% equity, few lenders will require PMI. At 22% equity the law requires that PMI be stopped, with the caveat that you have to ask.

Real estate agents (who are really just businesspeople trying to make a buck like any other) are notorious for steering homebuyers to homes they can afford *on paper*, but not in the real world. When banks (often working with real estate agents who have steered clients their way) pre-qualify a potential borrower, they often pre-qualify them for amounts they could only afford if they quit eating. Naturally, the real estate agent will suggest the "most amount of home" the borrower can "afford." It's incumbent on you not to fall into this trap. Once the papers are signed, the real estate agent will move on. If it turns out that you couldn't really afford the house after all, it's your problem. The real estate agent is neither your friend nor your adversary, but someone with whom you do business. Don't feel bad if you see a disappointed look in her eyes when you say no. It's just business.

Many times it is not the real estate agent or the bank who harms us, but the person who stares back at us from the mirror each morning. Sometimes desire overrides all reason.

When I was a kid my father took me to look at a car I had seen in a classified ad. It was love at first sight for me. I could picture myself cruising the open road and laughing at all those kids in school who would be dying of jealousy because I had my own car and they didn't. My father didn't look nearly so enthusiastic. The car had faded paint and some rust.

The guy selling the car asked if I wanted to take it for a test drive. I couldn't get into the driver's seat fast enough. The guy got into the passenger seat, and my father climbed into the back seat. I started the car. Other than the fact that it needed a new muffler, I couldn't see a problem. I could tell my father was skeptical about this car. He, apparently, was not seeing the same potential in this car that I was.

I drove around the neighborhood. The car would probably ride great once it got new tires. The engine was a little sluggish and knocked and pinged, but that was no big deal. All I had to do was put premium gas in it. This car was *the one*.

Suddenly, about two blocks away from the guy's house, the engine quit. I tried to restart it, but the engine wouldn't turn over. The guy reached over and turned the key. It wouldn't start for him either.

"It's probably just flooded," the guy said. "Let's just wait a few minutes."

"Let's go, Tommy," my father, no longer able to contain his annoyance, said as he threw open the door.

"But Dad, it's probably just flooded," I protested. I wanted this car. Whatever the matter was could be fixed.

"This car is a piece of junk. Let's go!"

The guy looked embarrassed, but said nothing. What could he say? My father was obviously right. We walked back to my father's car which was parked in front of the guy's house, then left. My father laughed as we pulled away, and told me he knew the car was a piece of junk the second he laid eyes on it. There was no way he was going to let me buy that car, even if it had run like a champ.

"Be a little bit patient," he told me. The right car for me was out there. We just had to find it. We did soon after. Dad liked *that* car so much that he soon confiscated it from me when his old car died!

Many first time homebuyers find themselves falling in love with a particular house despite some serious flaws. In the same way I fell in love with that car, some people will become so infatuated that they will overlook just about anything. In retrospect, I am glad my father was there to talk some sense into me.

Many homebuyers, being adults, don't have a voice of reason to talk them out of making a terrible decision.

The chief flaw is often that the house being considered is just unaffordable. We contort everything (as do the bank and real estate agent) to make the numbers work, but we know, deep down, that the numbers don't work. It's very easy to become enamored with that cute little three bedroom rancher, but it's not the only cute little three bedroom rancher in the world. If your credit score is not high enough to get you the most favorable terms, work on it awhile longer. If you don't have 20% to put down, save for another year or two. A house is not like a magazine or a pair of shoes you buy on impulse. It is a life-changing purchase. There is nothing wrong with waiting until the right house at the right time comes along. The real estate agent may make you feel as if you need to act *now*, but you don't. There will be other houses for sale later. Interest rates, while they may go up a little, are not headed into the stratosphere any time soon. Successful investing, real estate or otherwise, requires the ability to sometimes say no to yourself.

Definitely don't make the mistake that I would have surely made had my father not saved me from myself. A "fixer-upper" should only be purchased by people who actually have the ability to fix things up. Sometimes people will look at a house that needs work and, because of the cheap price, decide it's the one. They will learn to be handy, they tell themselves, or that their buddy's brother-in-law is a pretty good amateur carpenter. Don't do it! You may not have the aptitude to become a handyman. Your buddy's brother-in-law might not even be on speaking terms with him!

Always rent for at least a year if you are relocating to another part of the country. You may decide you hate the place so much that you quit your job to move back home. I have a sneaking suspicion that many of the people who've moved to North Dakota to get in on the oil boom in recent years are not finding those North Dakota winters to be to their liking.

To understand the Great Recession is to understand everything that can go wrong with real estate investing on a grand scale. In order to do that, it's necessary to go back to the very beginning.

The very beginning is 1977. This was the year the Community Reinvestment Act became law. The Community Reinvestment Act was enacted to remedy pervasive discrimination in lending against people (mostly minorities) living in "undesirable" neighborhoods. "Redlining," an egregious practice where red lines were drawn on maps to separate neighborhoods that were "good" for business from those that were "bad" for business was widespread. It was also blatantly and unconscionably racist. Well-qualified borrowers who lived in the "wrong" neighborhoods were routinely denied loans given to less well-qualified applicants who lived in the "right" neighborhoods. Those borrowers from the "wrong" neighborhoods who did manage to get loans almost always got them with terrible terms. They were, in other words, routinely ripped-off. Something had to be done, legally, ethically, and morally. The Community Reinvestment Act was that something. Unfortunately, for as well-intentioned as the law was, the results would ultimately be catastrophic. In a bitter irony, the people the law was intended to help were frequently the ones who got hurt the most.

Redlining was quickly replaced with "reverse redlining." The banks were well aware that, even if some people given loans in poor neighborhoods couldn't or wouldn't pay, most would. Homeowners in poor neighborhoods are no different than homeowners anywhere else. They will cut-down on food or not go to the doctor if it means keeping their homes. Completely irresponsible people don't normally have the inclination to go through the loan application process with its fees and constant demands for supporting documents. The universally terrible terms these loans came with ensured the banks would make money. Some of these terms were outrageous. A customer who wanted to pay-off his or her loan early or make additional principal payments would be hit with a "pre-payment penalty." A new term soon entered the English language. In 31 years it would be known to everybody. This term was "predatory lending."

Mainstream America didn't give too much thought to this thing we now call predatory lending over the next three decades. It was happening all the while, but as long as it didn't affect those with any real political power no one (except the victims) really seemed to care.

Then one day some unknown diabolical genius came up with an idea. It was an idea that was to bring down the whole rotten house of cards it was to spawn. It almost brought down the entire American economy. We are still suffering the effects of this wicked scheme.

This evil genius came up with a plan, at once brilliant and monstrous, to pass *all* the risk inherent in predatory lending to gullible investors. Preferably, these gullible investors would be foreign investors with a poor understanding of American financial markets and lots and lots of money.

CDOs (collateralized debt obligations) had existed for a long time, but our diabolical genius found a new way to use them. CDOs are securities that are bundled together (sort of like mutual funds) and sold as a package. Instead of shares of stock, however, CDOs contain debts. It was not at all uncommon for mortgage debt to be packaged into CDOs. Mortgage debt had historically been a fairly safe bet. People will generally do whatever it takes to not lose their houses. This evil genius realized that foreign investors would be unable to distinguish between prime and subprime debt if it was carefully hidden in a CDO.

Banks could suddenly make a lot more money in the subprime market with almost no additional risk. They did this by introducing the "no income verification" "stated income," or "liar" loan. Banks make a lot of money in fees in the mortgage writing process. They also make a lot of money by selling mortgages. If you've bought a home within the last 20 years chances are your mortgage has been sold a few times already. Banks, up until this point, had been very careful about writing mortgages. Though a foreclosed house can be resold, it is nearly always a loser for the bank. CDOs made this no longer an issue. The mortgage, bad or not, would soon be the problem of some unsuspecting investor in Shanghai or Taipei.

As with all bubbles before the burst, mania ensued. Housing prices soon became uncoupled from all reason. Houses were *doubling* in value within a year in places like Nevada, Florida, and California. Everywhere else they were going up by merely absurd, as opposed to insane, percentages. Mortgages were given out like candy at Halloween. A house could be bought for no money down. Liar loans proliferated. It didn't really matter to the bank if you said you were making $100,000 a year as a clerk at a convenience store. The loan officer would approve the loan with a wink and a nod, knowing the mortgage would be packed-up in a CDO and promptly sent to Asia.

When the whole rotten scheme came crashing down, as it was bound to do from the start, the carnage was horrific. Iconic American companies such as Bear Stearns and Washington Mutual did not survive 2008. AIG and General Motors almost certainly would have gone under had the government not bailed them out. Where credit flowed like water, it suddenly dried up, the tap cut-off by the same hand that had opened it wide.

There was no shortage of blame to be passed around. Everyone involved shared in it. The banks that packaged the CDOs were an obvious target, as were the rating agencies that certified these pieces of garbage as sound investments. The government had no business pushing homeownership onto people who were not ready for it, as if owning a home was some kind of civic duty. Finally, there were the borrowers. Many media outlets have given the borrowers a free pass, but I won't. Anyone who signs a contract is presumably an adult, but many people sure didn't act that way. Did anyone really believe their $500,000 house would be worth $16,000,000 in five years? Was everybody so drunk they thought the party would go on forever? Though many people like to blame greedy bankers and Wall Street crooks for the miserable economy we enjoy today, a good look in the mirror reveals an additional culprit in many cases.

Just as the physical damage to Europe from World War II wasn't completely repaired until the 1980s, the aftermath of the Great Recession is all around us today. Half-built housing developments with rotting McMansions litter the countryside in many places. Foreclosed and abandoned houses have turned formerly nice suburban neighborhoods into eyesores. Mostly vacant strip malls stand like monuments to life before the apocalypse throughout the country.

The human toll has been (and continues to be) severe. Millions of people are "underwater." They owe $300,000 for houses now appraised at $150,000. Many of these underwater homeowners have simply walked away. They now face the prospect of starting over from scratch, their credit ratings decimated, the threat of legal action sometimes hanging over their heads.

As credit dried-up like an arroyo in the desert after a deluge, companies, at first just cautious, started hoarding money. They did this by cutting spending to the bone. Tragically, much of these cuts were accomplished by cutting staff, many of whom had worked for the company for decades. It has now become a way of corporate life. Some of the employees have moved on to different jobs, but others, particularly older workers, continue to find the job search fruitless. We now find ourselves in a national economic catch-22: companies won't hire because consumers won't spend; consumers won't spend because companies won't hire.

There is one byproduct of the Great Recession that is likely a real structural economic change. If this is the case, the future does not bode well for the consumer society. It's quite possible that Millennials, those people born between 1982 and 2004, are adopting the ways of their great-grandparents. Like these ancestors who are survivors of the Great Depression and World War II, they have seen economic hardship (and many also war) up close. These young adults have graduated into the worst job market in generations, many with crushing student loan debts and few prospects. Although smug Baby Boomers and Generation X'ers call them a generation of "slackers," they have had it very much rougher than either of these two generational cohorts. In this they are like their great-grandparents. They don't live at home because they want to, but because they have to.

The danger for all of us is that Millennials will follow their great-grandparents' example and become a generation whose hallmarks are thrift and frugality. It's already happening. Although Millennials are not marrying or buying houses simply because they can't afford to, they are already changing one facet of American life. They are eschewing cars. Many of them don't care to drive; they would rather Facebook on their phones while riding the bus. If Millennials decide to become frugalists *en masse* as their great-grandparents did, the transition from a consumer economy will be a long and painful one.

There is no right or wrong answer as to whether or not one *should* buy a house. It's all a matter of personal preference. Financially, it's a wash or better if the renter wants it to be. My father used to say that renters were throwing their money away. I disagree. Renting puts a roof over your head without maintenance worries. Renting gives you a freedom to just get up and go homeowners don't enjoy. Homeownership, on the other hand, gives you roots. It gives you choice. Dogs are allowed if you decide they're allowed. The fact that a 30 year fixed mortgage usually becomes less burdensome over time is also very compelling. There is no right answer other than the one you choose.

Chapter Seven Takeaways

- There are pros and cons to renting versus buying.

- The old conventional wisdom that buying is clearly superior to renting is dead.

- Should you decide to buy, wait for the house you want and can truly afford.

- Most wealthy people own their home because they prefer the perceived security of homeownership.

VIII

Taxable Investing: The Arena of Joy and Pain

Taxable investing is the stadium where home runs (and sometimes grand slams) are hit, and where the losing team goes home in tears. Multi-million dollar contracts are negotiated and signed in the offices of this stadium, and there are many tragedies as well. Sometimes a fan will fall from the upper deck to his death or an old man will expire from natural causes during the seventh inning stretch. It can be a boring place as batter after batter is retired amidst a pitcher's duel, but the boredom seldom lasts for long. Eventually it will be supplanted by euphoria or unadulterated horror. This is no place for the clueless. They are soon exposed as the sheep among wolves they are. This is a place of both strategy and chance. Occasionally, there is a stolen base, very rarely a triple play. Sometimes a fan pulls a ball out of play or an unexpected gust of wind pushes a foul ball into fair territory. For those who play in this stadium, injuries are common. In fact, everybody gets hurt at some point or other. Many of these injuries are career-ending, some life-altering. One thing is for certain: you do not play in this league without serious preparation. Amateurs and the unprepared are slaughtered here every single day.

Taxable investing is investing outside of tax-advantaged accounts such as 401(k)s, 403(b)s, and IRAs. It is extremely dangerous for the reckless, but can also be lucrative beyond a person's wildest dreams. While there are many 401(k) millionaires, the taxable investing realm sometimes produces *billionaires*. Nearly all rich people have taxable investments in addition to retirement accounts.

Some of these wealthy people have no idea what they're invested in. They pay professionals to make their investment decisions for them and often don't give them much thought. A substantial number of rich people, on the other hand, are rich *precisely because* they have made taxable investments that have paid-off big time.

The conventional wisdom among financial advisors is that all debts (with the possible exception of your mortgage) should be paid-off and retirement accounts (including a 401(k) *and* a Roth IRA) fully funded before you put a penny into taxable investments. This is sound logic. With every conceivable type of investment available to the IRA investor, there is simply no *good* reason to play in the taxable arena unless you essentially have more money than you know what to do with. Why then, if taxable investing is illogical for most people and there are so many more losers than winners, do people do it?

For the chance to knock the ball out of the park.

Perhaps it is a misnomer to paint all the people who have taxable investments with the broad brush of "investor," though there are investors within this group to be sure. It might be more accurate to group those who play in this space as "investors" and "traders." (There is a third group, the speculators, but these are really just gamblers; they *always* lose in the long run.) The key difference between investors and traders is that investors usually make money while traders frequently lose their shirts. "Frequently" and "always" are not mutually exclusive terms, however. Some traders, albeit a tiny sliver of the total number, make *a lot* of money.

Stocks are the primary, but by no means only, financial instruments traders trade.

Day trading stocks got a well-deserved bad reputation after the technology bubble collapsed in 2000. Prior to that, some people were making hundreds or even thousands of dollars a day trading intra-day. They would buy a stock, wait for it to go up a few pennies, then dump it. They would do this over and over and over again. It was pretty easy when stocks, already overvalued, were being bid-up by the frenzied masses. John Maynard Keynes' "greater fool theory" was in full effect. All you needed to do was to find a greater fool than you to buy the piece of junk you had bought just seconds before. It wasn't hard.

Warren Buffett, the greatest investor who has ever lived (and no trader by any stretch of the imagination) has said the optimum holding period for a stock is "forever." The average share of stock, even today, is held for 22 *seconds*. Can you name the day trader who eclipsed Warren Buffett in wealth to become the world's second richest man? Neither can I.

It is entirely possible to make a good living trading stocks, but there is a major catch-22: you need to have *at least* $100,000 to do it, although $1,000,000 is much better. One thing the aspiring trader would be wise to keep in mind is that only a handful of people (Buffett chief among them) have ever beaten the long-term market averages consistently. Only 14% of actively managed mutual funds have beaten the market indices over the last 10 years. This is a pretty good advertisement for investing in cheap index funds and a pretty stern warning about the perils of trading! Still, just matching the market average (with the caveat that some years will be stellar and others dismal) would get you $9,400 a year with a $100,000 trading balance (not a bad part-time job in my opinion, but not really a living). A million dollars would get you $94,000 a year. (Now we're talking!) The problem is, where do you get a million dollars to fund your brokerage account? Oh, those damned catch-22s . . .

The biggest difference between the typical investor or trader and the speculator is "due diligence." Due diligence is the process of studying a security and making an educated guess based on your findings. Warren Buffett starts his due diligence with the premise that when you buy a stock you are really buying a business. One of the key reasons Buffett has done so well over the years is that, while it's not possible to know if a company is a bargain without delving further into the metrics of the stock, it is possible to tell a good company from an utterly unknown one. Peter Lynch, the legendary manager of Fidelity's *Magellan Fund* (which under his tenure was the world's largest and most successful mutual fund) lives by the motto "invest in what you know." Buffett has always invested this way. When the financial pundits were declaring that Buffett had "lost his touch" in the late 90s because he avoided technology stocks he couldn't understand, he looked even more brilliant when the market tanked. Suddenly those "lame" carpet makers, brick makers, soda companies, and banks didn't seem so lame after all.

Everybody loses. Warren Buffett has stated that Berkshire Hathaway (the Massachusetts textile manufacturer he acquired in the 1960s whose name he would keep for his conglomerate) was a big mistake. Buffett has, he freely admits, made plenty of others. Shrewd investors understand, however, that singles can get you into the Hall of Fame; singles hitters, alas, also strike out quite often.

The best stock traders, like the best stock investors, also practice due diligence. Where "momentum traders" (who are really just speculators) will find a rapidly rising stock they know little or nothing about and buy it in the hope it will keep going up for another 22 seconds, the best stock traders are not necessarily *day* traders. They may hold their stocks for a day, a week, a month, or a year. One object of trading stocks is to make money. Another is not losing money. The *first* rule of stock trading is to cut your losses. This doesn't mean dumping a quality stock because it goes down in price by a buck or two, but knowing when to take your lumps and lick your wounds. A speculative stock that loses half its value needs to rise *100%* just to break even. Research into financial psychology has discovered that most of us are at terrible at knowing when to quit. The futile hope that our stock will "come back" frequently overrides our common sense. Wise traders know that it is always better to "dump your dogs" and "let your winners run."

There are many methods for choosing which stocks to buy and which to avoid. The worst form of "due diligence," in my opinion, is to buy or sell based on analyst opinion. As I wrote earlier, I have seen "strong buy" and "strong sell" recommendations on the same stock on the same day by two different analysts. They couldn't both be right. I once made the costly mistake of buying a stock because it had "strong buy" recommendations from several analysts. It was, admittedly, a speculative stock, but it seemed (at the time) that nothing could possibly go wrong. When I finally dumped the stock a month later at a 30% loss, I realized that maybe due diligence based solely on analyst opinion was a little bit *too* easy. It certainly didn't work. Just a note here about the importance of dumping losers: the stock eventually went to zero. I definitely got stung, but it could have been much worse.

As I *never* bet against Warren Buffett, the first step in due diligence should be finding out if the company you are thinking of buying stock in is a quality company. A company doesn't need to be a household name to be a solid company, but a "moat" (a competitive advantage that provides a margin of safety) is never a bad thing. Understanding what the company *does* is crucial. Peter Lynch probably would have recommended McDonald's over Enron because selling hamburgers is much easier to understand than energy trading. (Enron, by the way, collapsed in grand style, bankrupting some of its investors and destroying the 401(k)s of its employees who were required to hold large amounts of Enron stock. The only good thing to come out of the whole fiasco was that a law was passed where companies could no longer require employees to hold company stock.)

Both the serious individual stock investor or trader and the dabbler would be very wise to learn something about accounting. Accounting is the language of business. Due diligence requires the ability to at least read a company's balance sheet and income statement. *Accounting For Dummies* may not be as exciting a read as *Fifty Shades of Gray*, but dollar for dollar, it can give you a much bigger bang for the buck!

The Internet has changed investing in ways that are paradoxically good and bad. There is a lot of information out there. For people who learn to sift the gold from the dirt this information is like free money, but for many others it is a minefield and a source of paralysis.

Back in the old days, when few regular people messed around with stocks, information was hard to come by. What information one could get from the *Wall Street Journal* or *Businessweek* was stale as soon as it was published. In her excellent book *The Snowball: Warren Buffett and the Business of Life*, Alice Schroeder paints a vivid picture of a young Warren Buffett holed-up in a room on a Friday night pouring over issues of *Standard & Poor's Stock Guide* looking for bargains. My how times have changed.

Now it is possible to watch the movement of a stock in real time. Numerous websites now exist that provide volumes of information for free. Online brokerages provide their clients with information the young Warren Buffett could only dream of. This includes buy or sell recommendations for specific stocks and the metrics of most stocks. The metrics of a stock are at the heart of due diligence. The smart investor or trader looks closely at these numbers.

It is impossible to know the future (which is why the stock trading "systems" peddled in infomercials are a bunch of bull), but there are certain clues about a company that can be gleaned from the metrics. Publicly-traded companies are required by law to make some information public. There is a method known as "technical analysis" for making an educated guess about a stock. This methodology was laid-out in Benjamin Graham's (Warren Buffett's mentor and professor at Columbia University) earth-shattering (but very boring sounding) book *Security Analysis* (co-written by David Dodd), and further explained in his even better book, *The Intelligent Investor*.

I won't even begin to try to get into the details of technical analysis here (Graham's book *The Intelligent Investor* has no equal and should be read by anyone who trades), but it boils down to this: "Mr. Market," a traveling salesman, comes to your door at the same time every day offering to sell you his product (a stock). Some days the price is too high and you tell him "no thanks" before closing the door in his face. Some days the price is just right. You can buy or not. Mr. Market will never pressure you. Some days, however, the price is just too good to pass up. There are many reason why this might be so, but, if the company is intrinsically sound, you can rest assured this cheap price will not last. Technical analysis is the thing that enables you to make the best guess possible about Mr. Market's offering for that day.

While price is key, I like to know a company is solvent. A cheap price is meaningless if the product is a falling knife. My own personal method for deciding whether or not a stock is too risky is to read the company's balance sheet. With the very important warning that things can change a lot since a balance sheet was last made public (usually at the end of the year), a balance sheet, more than anything else, reveals a company's health. A balance sheet tells you what long- and short-term assets a company has, as well as long-term and short-term liabilities. I like to see that a company has short-term assets greater than *total* liabilities. This means that the company can ride-out a short-term storm. It also means that, in the worst case scenario that the company goes out of business, investors will get *something* when the assets are liquidated. John A. Tracy's book *Accounting For Dummies* (which is as readable and interesting as a book on accounting can possibly be) explains how to read and understand a balance sheet very succinctly.

Another document companies release that is profoundly useful is the income statement. I like to see that a company has some money left over after operating expenses. In fact, the more the better. Tracy's book also explains the income statement in a way non-accounting majors can understand.

Finally, I always look at a stock's beta. Beta is a measure of volatility. A beta of 1.0 is exactly as volatile as the market. Anything higher is more volatile, anything lower less. All things considered, less volatility is better. One odd reality of the trading world is that the boring nerds almost always beat the "exciting" Wall Street "players" in the end. I'm sure there were plenty of Wall Street guys out drinking martinis and smoking cigarettes with gorgeous "dames" those Friday nights Buffett was home reading the *Standard & Poor's Stock Guide*!

There is nothing wrong with buying quality. In fact, some highly successful traders increase their fortunes strictly by buying excellent companies when they're having a bad day. (The companies, not the traders!) When Boeing's stock took a hit as a result of battery fires in the company's new 787 "Dreamliner" it was a foregone conclusion that the engineers would come up with a fix. The company had put way too much money into research and development to simply give up. If the engineers at NASA could get Apollo 13 home safely using only what the astronauts had on board the craft, it was a pretty good bet the engineers at Boeing could figure out a way to fix the battery problems on the Dreamliner. They did. The stock recovered nicely and the traders booked their (in retrospect) easy profits.

Many speculators, most of whom quickly go broke, look for the big score. Trading penny stocks is a great way to lose your money fast. Penny stocks are stocks that trade for cheap (not to be confused with inexpensive) prices, usually under five bucks a share but often literally for pennies. These stocks are most often traded "over the counter" or on the "pink sheets," that is, not on a major stock exchange like the New York Stock Exchange or the Nasdaq. While the prospect of buying 10,000 shares of stock for a dime apiece and making a quick 500 bucks when they go up a nickel a share sounds good (and sells a lot of newsletters with the "hot" names), penny stocks are penny stocks for a reason. The underlying businesses are often lousy or barely existent. A quick look at the balance sheets and the income statements often tell you all you need to know. Penny stocks traded over the counter are not subject to the same regulations as companies listed on the major stock exchanges. Perhaps most dangerously, penny stocks are frequently "illiquid" or "thinly-traded."

When you buy or sell a stock, you execute a trade through a brokerage such as Scottrade, TD Ameritrade, or Trade King. There must be a willing buyer and a willing seller for a trade to happen. The brokerage's job is to match you, the buyer, with a seller or vice versa. In the case of a large company stock like

Chevron, IBM. or Delta Airlines, the transaction is almost instantaneous. Most other transactions are completed within well under a minute. The problem with thinly-traded stocks is that there may simply not be a buyer when you go to sell. Most brokerages charge much higher commissions to trade penny stocks compared to more liquid stocks with higher market capitalizations.

While you could make a fortune trading penny stocks, you could also make a fortune playing high stakes blackjack in a casino. The casino is more fun, however, and the drinks are free!

Just a note of caution: a price under five dollars a share does not necessarily mean a stock is a penny stock. There is, in fact, a lot of opportunity in this space for the trader with a higher risk tolerance. At the depths of the 2008 bear market, stocks such as Ford were trading for under three dollars a share. Some very sound regional banks that actually pay dividends can still be had at super-low prices. The key to finding them is due diligence.

One type of stock that can frequently be found under five dollars a share is the pharmaceutical or biotechnology stock. These stocks, while not all penny stocks, come with the particular danger of having only one product that must be approved by the government for sale. You could make a fortune if you pick the small company that gets FDA approval to market an experimental drug, but keep in mind that only one in 5,000 drug ideas ever make it to market. It is far safer to invest in large companies like Merck, Johnson & Johnson, or Novartis with tons of cash and several products in the pipeline at any given time.

Although the Internet has made investing and trading information vastly easier to come by with sites such as Morningstar, Yahoo Finance, MSN Money, and CNN Money (as well as brokerage costs to plummet), trading and investing, unless you are really just a gambler, takes work. Wealthy people understand that making an educated guess about which stocks to buy takes a lot of research beforehand. Wealthy active traders and successful investors spend hours reading news (which can have a profound effect on a particular stock or the entire market), reading balance sheets and income statements, and looking for trends. A lot of affluent people pay good money to have this research done for them. Despite all this, everybody loses sometimes.

Most working people who trade do so as a hobby. There is nothing inherently wrong with this as long as rent and/or retirement money is not what's being traded. It still takes due diligence. Understand that professionals have all day to do research and powerful computer programs that can influence entire markets. In May 2010 computers caused stocks to plummet in a "flash crash" that lasted only minutes, but cost investors with "stop loss" orders (where stocks are automatically sold if they sink to a predetermined price chosen by the investor) dearly. Do your homework. Read the "investor information" brokerages post on their websites. Read the free articles on the financial sites mentioned above, and pick up a copy of *Money* or *Kiplinger's Personal Finance* every once in awhile. Definitely read *The Intelligent Investor*. Learn the terminology. Knowledge is power. The best traders and investors know this. Now you do too.

One relatively safe and effective way to enter the taxable investing sphere is to start with good old-fashioned mutual funds. Most mutual fund families have onerous minimums for non-retirement investors, but a few will let you start with nothing if you agree to allow them to debit at least $100 a month from your checking account. You will have to keep this up until you meet the $2,500 or $3,000 minimum balance requirement, but you will be dollar cost averaging the entire time. Unlike in retirement accounts, you will have to pay taxes on dividends and capital gains each year, but there is no penalty for early withdrawal if you want to get your hands on this money before age 59 ½. Mutual funds are way safer than individual stocks because of their built-in diversity. I have never heard of a mutual fund going to zero, but I have personally owned two stocks that did just that!

Just as many stock traders swing for the fences, so too do some taxable mutual fund investors. A person may decide to put a few thousand dollars into a somewhat speculative investment with the hopes of cashing-in big and fast, but may not have the risk tolerance of the pure speculator. These investments might be whole sectors such as precious metals, oil, emerging or frontier markets, or "inverse" market funds (funds that go up when stock markets go down). Though there are no guarantees you'll make money (or that you won't *lose* money), mutual funds are a far safer way to play sectors than buying individual stocks.

The guy I mentioned before who collects investments the same way some people collect stamps started with mutual funds outside the ones he held in his 401(k). He funded his first taxable investments with automatic monthly withdrawals from his checking account, kicking-in whatever extra he could from tax refunds or overtime. He did this for several years. When he had built-up a large enough sum, he opened a brokerage account and bought his first individual stocks. He has never looked back, but still (he informs me) has his first taxable mutual funds.

Another option for people with enough money to make opening a brokerage account worthwhile, but who nevertheless crave the safety and diversity of mutual funds, is the ETF. ETF is short for "exchange-traded fund." Exchange-traded funds are just like mutual funds in that they can contain scores, hundreds, or even thousands of stocks in a single share, but trade on an exchange just like an individual stock. You can buy just one share and forget about it if you like. You can buy 100 shares at 10:00 o'clock, and sell them all at noon. Some people will divert profits from an individual stock trade into an ETF as a way of booking profits. Some mutual fund families, such as Vanguard, offer ETFs that are essentially the same thing as their mutual funds, only with no minimums and lower expense ratios. The only drawback to ETFs is that you pay a commission when you buy, and another commission when you sell. Some mutual fund families that also offer brokerage services, however, will let you trade their ETFs commission-free! In this case, ETFs are the closest thing to the perfect investment that exists.

Whether you choose ETFs, individual stocks, or a combination of the two for your brokerage account, you don't need to actively trade (as fun and exciting as trading can sometimes be). Though some brokerages have "inactivity fees," it's easy enough to find one that doesn't. Most brokerages will allow you to reinvest the dividends you earn. You'll recall that Warren Buffett said the optimal holding period for a stock is "forever."

Despite the fact that any good financial advisor will beat the drum of diversity incessantly (for the very good reason that a diversified portfolio provides a large margin of safety), most very rich investors get that way by concentrating their holdings. Buffett didn't make his billions by owning broad-market index funds, but large quantities of a relatively few individual stocks. He held those stocks "forever" for the most part. Those times his stocks were down, he bought more and took comfort in the knowledge he was getting paid to wait because those stocks paid dividends. Unlike the trader, the investor must learn and practice the very valuable art of patience.

I personally know some otherwise "Average Joes" who have built fortunes relative to their peers by simply buying an individual stock or two and holding on for decades. One guy who gave me permission to tell his story illustrates the power of a concentrated holding of an excellent stock perfectly.

"Jay" got an insert with his water bill back in 1992 offering to sell customers stock in the utility directly at a 15% discount. Though he had an IRA, Jay had never owned an individual stock in his life. He was intrigued, but nervous. He had just gotten a $1,400 tax refund. (Jay is a thrifty guy; money does not burn a hole in his pocket.) He mulled it over. He had no idea about due diligence, but a water company seemed like a fairly safe bet. People need water and are not likely to go back to using communal wells or drawing water out of the river in order to save a buck. He executed. He mailed in the insert with a check for the entire $1,400.

Today, Jay's biggest regret is that he didn't buy more. He never added a single cent to his original $1,400, but that $1,400 has grown to well over $30,000. Jay tells me he will never sell it because he has "fallen in love" with this "childhood sweetheart" of stocks. Normally, it's a bad idea to fall in love with your stocks (because it makes it harder to dump losers), but in Jay's case it worked out.

As in Jay's case, not all stocks need to be purchased through a broker. "DRIP" (dividend reinvestment program) stocks are sold by many high quality companies directly to the public. Usually, you just print the investment form from the company website, fill it out, and mail it in with your check. Though you will pay taxes on the dividends, you will not pay capital gains taxes until you sell your shares and the gains are "realized" many years later.

DRIPs are a great way for the person who has a little extra money and doesn't want to trade to get a piece of the taxable investing action. DRIPs are a great present for kids, but bear in mind that any money you put into your kid's name can have an adverse effect on future college financial aid. As with any other stock purchase, DRIPs require due diligence, but many of the companies that sell their stock directly are solid, well-known companies.

Taxable investing, as mentioned at the beginning of this chapter, can be an extremely dangerous thing. There are a plethora of "investments" out there that are not only supremely risky, but cannot even justify the risk with appreciably better returns than you could get with a plain-vanilla index fund.

One of the biggest dangers out there is not an investment, but an enticement offered by brokerages. Margin accounts are lines of credit offered by brokerages that enable the investor to borrow money to buy securities. DON'T DO IT! The only thing that needs to be said about margin accounts is don't have one. There is possibly nothing worse than losing your money on a stock, then having to pay back the money you borrowed to buy the loser when there is a sudden "margin call." Just don't do it.

You may have heard the term "short selling." "Shorting" a stock is betting that the price will fall. It works like this: you think XYZ company's stock price will fall. You borrow a thousand shares from your broker. You don't owe the brokerage money per se, you owe them a thousand shares of XYZ stock. You sell the shares immediately. The price falls. You take the proceeds from the sale, pay back the brokerage, and pocket the difference. Life is good. What happens if the stock price rises? You owe the brokerage 1,000 shares of XYZ. What if XYZ becomes the next Berkshire Hathaway overnight? You go broke in grand style. The problem with shorting stocks is that, unlike buying a stock that goes to zero and where you lose your entire investment, there is no limit to how much you can lose short selling. If you absolutely must dabble in shorts, do it through an inverse mutual fund with a tiny fraction of your portfolio.

The average investor can do quite well without trading in options, futures, and foreign currencies, thank you very much. The big banks that trade currency have better software than you do. Trading options and futures has all the features of gambling, but very little of the fun that can be had on a good night at the casino. Really, what is the difference between betting that the corn crop will be bad due to drought or that the winter will be cold, as opposed to betting that your 20 will beat whatever the dealer has because she's showing a six? Free drinks and more fun is all I can see.

The taxable investing world, while perilous, can be very profitable. The critical factor is due diligence. The taxable investor would be wise to learn and practice it.

Chapter Eight Takeaways

- Taxable investing can be lucrative, but comes with serious risk.

- Traders sometimes win big, but often lose even bigger.

- Patient investors generally make money.

- Learn the art of "due diligence" in order to make the most educated guesses possible.

- Invest in what you know.

- Accounting is the language of business.

- ETFs are like mutual funds and individual stocks rolled into one.

- Concentrating gives potentially bigger gains (and losses) than diversifying.

- It is possible to buy some stocks directly from the company.

- Never buy on margin, period!

- There are just some investments you don't need.

IX

Keep What You've Got

In 1986 I had the most expensive dinner I ever had. It took two years to complete and made a real mess of the kitchen. To add insult to injury, I never did get to eat it.

I was sharing an apartment with my cousin at the time. I had no idea he was a worse cook than me (or that such a thing was even possible). I had picked up some breaded chicken patties on my way home from work, and, on his instructions, put them on a baking sheet and threw them in the oven. I went out to the living room to play a few games of "Moon Patrol," then, 30 minutes or so later, went back to the kitchen. The chicken patties were stone-cold. The oven wasn't working. I started saying a few choice words about our cheapskate landlord. My cousin told me to calm down; there was another way to cook them. All I had to do was fill-up a pan with oil, bring it to a boil on the range, and drop the chicken patties in until they turned a nice golden brown. I had no way to know that catastrophe was about to ensue. I followed his directions to the letter, and figured I would go get in another quick game of Moon Patrol while the oil came to a boil.

I heard a *swoosh* like a blanket being shaken-out come from the kitchen. I went to investigate. At that very moment flames jumped from the pot to the wall and started climbing. The smoke detectors started screaming and the cat ran by. (We would later find him quivering under my cousin's bed.)

I froze in panic. My cousin grabbed a damp towel from the bathroom, ran back to the kitchen, and started beating the flames.

"Get everybody the hell out of here," he ordered. We lived in a quadplex and I ran to each of the neighbor's doors and told them to get out because the place was on fire. My other cousin, who lived in one of the other units, ran upstairs to help put out the flames while his wife called the fire department. The other neighbors, meanwhile, were looking at me with murder in their eyes.

The fire department arrived a few minutes later. My cousins had already put the fire out, but they inspected the place to make sure there was nothing smoldering. They left and my cousin and I started the long process of cleaning the place up.

Over the next few weeks we cleaned and painted the place, and waited for our landlord to replace the oven (which had caused this mess in the first place). Ironically, the range where the fire started was unscathed.; it was still usable, although I was now eating out for every meal. It would be a very long time before I would try my hand at cooking again. A few weeks later our landlord put in a new stove and bolted a metal plate to the wall next to the range. We figured that was the end of it. He couldn't be too mad at us because he was going to have to fix or replace the old stove anyway. A couple of months later he proceeded to put new siding on the building. This struck us as odd because he was so awful cheap, but we didn't think too much of it. Maybe he was turning over a new leaf and suddenly cared about his tenants. Little did we know what was coming.

The letter from the insurance company arrived soon after. We owed $5,800 for damages caused by the fire. I was outraged. How was this our problem? The landlord's stove wasn't working, and besides, we were only renters. We would have just ignored the letter and told them to go pound sand, but the letter stated that if we didn't pay up we would be sued in court. My cousin talked to my uncle (his father) about this. My uncle wasn't sure how to proceed, but had house counsel to advise him on business matters. He got us an appointment with the lawyer.

The first thing the lawyer told us was that there was no problem, because renter's insurance would cover the fire damage.

"What's renter's insurance?" I asked. My cousin didn't know what it was either.

The lawyer shook his head and stared at us in disbelief. "Don't tell me you guys don't have renter's insurance."

He could tell by our shameful looks that we didn't.

"You guys are going to lose in court," he informed us, matter-of-factly.

"Yeah, but we don't own the place," I said in my best TV courtroom argument voice. "Besides, his stove not working is what caused this mess in the first place."

"Doesn't matter. If you damage somebody's property, you have to pay for it. That's that."

"What are we going to do? We don't have $5,800," my cousin said.

"Well, the only thing you can do is try to get the number knocked-down by a judge," said the lawyer. "Did you do any of the clean-up yourselves?"

"Yes," my cousin said triumphantly.

"Can you prove it? Do you have pictures or receipts for supplies?"

"Both," my cousin said, as if adding the coup de grâce.

He had taken "before and after" pictures mainly so we could see what kind of job we had done. It just so happened we had a bag with a few extra paintbrushes and *all* of the receipts in it.

The lawyer drafted a letter to the insurance company asking them what they'd settle for.

"No dice," was their reply. They wanted the entire $5,800. The lawyer then drafted another letter to the effect of "see you in court."

A couple of months later the county sheriff came to our door and handed me a subpoena. My uncle arranged another meeting with the lawyer. He wouldn't be going to court with us, but coached us on what to say. The judge who would be hearing our case, he informed us, was a very no-nonsense man. We'd better not give him even a hint of attitude.

The day finally came. We put on suits and ties, and I told my cousin to let me do the talking.

The judge was a fierce looking man. He looked like he'd give you life without parole for jaywalking in a heartbeat. It was all I could do not to tremble in fear as he thundered down from the bench.

"Sir, where is your witness?" He was talking to the insurance company's lawyer who was sitting at a table opposite us, alone.

"He's not here yet, Your Honor," the lawyer answered sheepishly.

"Well, he'd better get here. Fast. Wasting my time won't do a thing for your case. Tell me your side of the story, young man," he said, turning his attention to me.

"Your Honor, we don't dispute that we're at fault in this case," I began. "What we are disputing is the amount of money owed. We did virtually all of the clean-up. We have pictures and receipts that will support our case." I wasn't doing half bad. Maybe all those reruns of Perry Mason I'd watched hadn't been such a bad use of my time after all.

The bailiff took the pictures and receipts and handed them to the judge. He examined them for what seemed like an hour, although it couldn't have been more than a few minutes. The courtroom was absolutely silent.

"These young men make a very valid point," the judge finally said. "What do you have to say about it?" The judge glared at the insurance company's lawyer.

"I can't really comment without my witness, Your Honor." The missing witness was none other than our landlord.

"There's no need to. Judgement for the defendants," he said, pounding his gavel suddenly. "Have a nice day, gentlemen. You boys don't owe a dime."

"Man, you were great! You're a better lawyer than that guy was," my cousin gushed on the ride home.

"Well, you know . . ." I said, puffing myself up like a rooster.

We moved on with our lives. We rarely thought about the fire, but concluded that the check meant to pay for the fire damage had instead bought some pretty nice siding.

I nearly passed out from shock when the sheriff returned with another subpoena.

The insurance company was appealing their loss. I didn't know what to do. We went back to my uncle's lawyer yet again.

"This is where the game gets interesting," he said. "You have already won once in court, but that's not a guarantee you'll win again. It's possible a different judge will make you pay the entire $5,800. On the other hand, the insurance company knows it's taking a calculated risk. They have already lost once. A different judge might be annoyed that they're wasting his time with this appeal. I recommend you settle. This is a matter of saving face for them now."

"But we don't have $5,800 to settle with," I protested. "It's a matter of face for us too. We did the work. We paid for the supplies. Why should we pay for the landlord's new siding too?"

"I didn't say you needed to settle for $5,800; just offer them something. Anything."

I sent them a letter certified mail, return receipt requested. We were offering $200 to make this thing go away. If they didn't accept it, we would go back to court. It was a matter of principle now.

A week later I got a certified letter back from the insurance company. It contained the address where I was to mail the check for $200. They had accepted our offer. It was over.

Though renter's insurance would have saved a lot of money and anxiety, I often shudder when I think back to how much worse this ordeal could have been. Aside from the fact that I would have never forgiven myself if someone had been killed or severely burned, this run-of-the-mill kitchen fire could have destroyed my life permanently in other ways.

The lawyer was absolutely right: I was legally responsible for the damages. Why I thought I shouldn't be held liable because I didn't own the place shows just how immature I still was at the time. It would be like saying someone who hits your car doesn't owe anything for damages because it's not *their* car. That may be perfect kid logic, but it's not how things work in the real world. I am quite sure that if the place had burned to the ground I would be paying for the rest of my life. Not only was the building worth more than most single family homes, but I would have also been on the hook for every bit of personal property in every one of the apartments.

There is an old saying "you can't squeeze blood from a stone." The context in which this expression is most often used is in talking about people who are sued for amounts they couldn't ever possibly pay. I certainly had nothing to take back then. Indeed, the insurance company couldn't have "squeezed blood from a stone." The problem would have been, had the worst case scenario occurred, that I would have had a judgement for hundreds of thousands of dollars against me. This would have ensured that I would never accumulate anything. Except for the minimum for bare survival, the courts might have confiscated every penny I made.

Although I certainly didn't feel lucky then, I realize now that I was profoundly lucky. My life would have been totally different (very much for the worse) had the fire gotten totally out of control.

Unfortunately for many working people, insurance is one of those things most people don't think about until it's too late. In fact, aside from car insurance which is legally required and health insurance which is usually still provided by one's employer as of 2014, most of us give very little thought to insurance at all. I had no concept that there even was such a thing as renter's insurance when I had my kitchen fire. It was as far from my thoughts as the weather in Mongolia. Such ignorance is not uncommon. Most of us don't know what to insure, let alone for how much. The idea that our ignorance could literally wreck our lives never even crosses our mind until the very real prospect is staring us in the face. One thing that was absolutely certain is that it was way too late to buy renter's insurance by the time I was thinking about it.

Nowhere is the chasm between the rich and everybody else wider than when it comes to insurance. Rich people insure their health, their cars, their homes, their lives, and above all, their wealth. They are well aware that what they worked, saved, and invested for could be lost in the blink of an eye. Few poor, working-, and middle class people, on the other hand, ever think about the one thing insurance could most prevent their losing–the opportunity for future prosperity.

Renter's insurance would have certainly covered the damages for the kitchen fire, but would have come nowhere near covering everything had the worst happened. Many everyday people have a poor understanding of liability. (I had no understanding of it whatsoever in 1986.) The state tells us we must have car insurance, but what is *required* and what is *enough* are two different things altogether. In some states the minimum legal coverage for property damage from a car accident is $5,000! A fender-bender could easily cost more than this. Total a garden variety car worth $20,000, and that puts the holder of such a policy on the hook for $15,000! Cause a chain reaction accident on the Garden State Parkway and it's all over. All this assumes only property damage; factor-in injuries or death and it gets much, much worse. Those insurance companies that advertise the minimum coverage required by law will, in fact, prevent their customers from getting a ticket, but that's about it. A $5,000 property damage limit will almost guarantee that you will *stay* a stone from which blood cannot be squeezed if you are at fault in a serious accident. Forever.

Knowing *how much* coverage you need is important, but knowing *what kind* of insurance you need should be part of the overall process of taking stock as you draw-up your roadmap to financial independence.

It was my great fortune to find a fantastic insurance agent right from the beginning. Paul was a friend of my father's, and as mean as a snake. He would sit at his desk in his office (which looked like it came straight out of a 1970s TV show about a private detective), chain smoking cigarettes and yelling at his customers over the phone. For as miserable as he was, he had a lot of clients. The reason for this is that he was brutally honest. He would sell you only what you needed, but at the same time, would refuse to write a policy he felt was inadequate, legal or not. He apparently didn't care a wit about making money for himself. If you told him you needed a car insurance policy at only the legal minimum, he would tell you to get lost. My favorite memory of Paul is when I was sitting at his desk as he wrote my homeowner's policy. The phone rang and he proceeded to tell whoever was on the other end of the line that they could either go to another insurance company or go to hell. He wouldn't write that policy. The call went on for quite awhile. I started getting bored and picked up a brochure called "Your Wood Stove and Your Insurance."

"Hold on a minute," Paul said. He pressed the phone into his shoulder to mute it, took a deep drag of his cigarette, snatched the brochure out of my hands, tore it up, and threw it on the floor.

"There's no goddamn way you're getting a wood stove, Tommy," he said gruffly before returning to the phone call.

Paul would have insisted that I get a renter's insurance policy had he known I was renting an apartment. He was the perfect insurance agent in that he would tell you *what* you needed and *how much* without trying to take you to the cleaners. Though he wouldn't sell you a policy he thought was inadequate, he wouldn't hesitate to say "you don't need that" either. (Paul has since passed away, but the guy who took over for him is also a pretty good insurance agent.)

In the same way that rich people hire and build relationships with accountants, financial advisors, and lawyers, having a good and trusted insurance agent can be invaluable. Insurance is the defense portion of your game plan. Any good football coach will tell you that a good defensive coordinator is worth his weight in gold. The same goes for having a good honest insurance agent.

Car insurance is the first insurance most of us ever seriously think about. As a nation historically in love with cars and the open road, this is the type of insurance most of us ever have to spend our own money on. Usually we are added as an extra driver on our parent's policies, but most parents require that we pay something as an additional lesson in responsibility. Most 16 year-olds will not have to worry about liability limits if they're on their parent's policies, but will quickly be reminded how expensive car insurance for a 16 year-old can be. Sixteen year-olds are expensive to insure for a very good reason. They have no experience and are statistically the most dangerous drivers. Add in texting and driving around with friends, and the results are sometimes disastrous. *All good parents make and enforce strict rules for teenaged drivers.*

For the average driver (and the younger driver in particular), there are a few ways to bring down the cost of car insurance. Passing a driver's ed program (which was mandatory when I was in high school) will almost always get you a discount. Many insurance companies will give a discount for good grades. There is a direct correlation between earning good grades and overall responsibility. Not getting tickets or having accidents is the obvious way to eventually get "safe driver" discounts.

All insurance comes with a deductible. This is the amount of money you have to pay out of pocket before insurance picks up the rest. Deductibles are usually $250, $500, or $1,000. The higher the deductible you can afford, the cheaper your premiums will be. Some people add extra money to their emergency funds to hedge against the possibility of a car accident. They raise their deductibles to this limit and, in the event they don't have an accident, collect interest on the "float." Float, the time between when insurance premiums are collected (and the money earning interest) and claims paid-out, was a big contributor to Warren Buffett's fortune!

While only liability insurance is required by states, banks that finance new cars require collision and comprehensive insurance for things such as theft, vandalism, and a tree branch crushing the car. This type of insurance is necessary for a new car, because there are few things worse than making payments on a car that has already been sent to the junkyard. The bank's logic is that someone whose car has been damaged or destroyed will not have quite the same motivation to pay-up as someone who is still basking in that new car smell. The key to collision and comprehensive insurance is knowing when to get rid of it.

With the possible exception of some 1930s collectible model in pristine condition, cars are depreciating assets. Their value goes steadily down until they are worth nothing. It doesn't matter how well you take care of your particular car, insurance companies look at "book value" when paying a claim. Say you have a 15 year old car that you have taken impeccable care of. The car runs great and is worth plenty as far as you're concerned. It's still a great car. One night a drag racer hits it when it is parked out on the street. The car is destroyed. You have faithfully paid your premiums for collision and comprehensive all these years. You figure you will just go down to the dealer on Saturday and pick out a new car. Your insurance agent informs you he has a check for the full book value of the totaled car to give you. You swing by the office to find the check is for $100! You have indeed been paid full "book value" for the car.

Generally, by the time a car is seven or eight years old, keeping collision and comprehensive insurance is just throwing money away.

The health insurance system in this country, which has been shameful for years, is now just a twisted mess of confusion. The "Affordable Care Act," a.k.a. "Obamacare," is having an extremely rough rollout at the time of this writing. Whether or not the ACA will do anything to improve what preceded it (which would have actually taken real effort to make any worse) remains to be seen. Early indications are the "Affordable Care Act" may not be all that affordable. This is causing business to proceed with caution in making hiring decisions. I can't say I blame them. Having no idea what future costs will be is not exactly good for business. Unfortunately, this uncertainty, more so than just cheapness on the part of business owners, is preventing many people who need and want full-time jobs from getting them.

The healthcare system in America is a direct byproduct of World War II. When employers were forbidden from giving their employees raises when price and wage freezes were implemented as part of the war effort, most employers compensated their employees by providing health insurance. This employer-provided health insurance soon became the norm. In the years after the war, having health insurance became contingent on having a full-time job. For the most part, it is still this way. Though it's possible the ACA could change this, for now unemployed and underemployed people just have to hope they don't get sick.

Disgracefully, the United States is the only civilized nation in the world where it is entirely possible to be bankrupted by medical bills even *with* health insurance. Only in America are you practically guaranteed to be harassed in your sickbed. The insurance lobby now so thoroughly owns Congress that they are the only industry that gets to decide *what* they will pay, *when* they will pay, or even *if* they will pay. Only in America are you virtually assured to be nickel-and-dimed after even a minor operation.

When it comes to healthcare, I am for a single-payer system. Call me a socialist if you will, but I don't think old people should have to buy additional "Part B" insurance or that working people should have to write nuisance checks to five different entities when all their procedures were done in the same hospital. All American citizens should be able to just show their medical card and be done with it. If taxes have to go up, even by a lot, to make this happen, so be it. We're all probably paying more than a good single-payer plan would cost right now anyway. Of course, you should be able to buy an insurance plan that covers the bells and whistles if you want. Countries like France and Australia have public-private healthcare systems that deliver far better outcomes for far less cost. I would wonder why we don't, but I already know the answer: big fat political campaign contributions.

My rant notwithstanding, you need health insurance for the same reason you need adequate car insurance. Many people are under the impression that people without health insurance go to the emergency room, get patched-up, and go on their merry way. This is not quite how it works. Sure, no one will be turned away from an emergency room who really needs medical treatment. The streets of America would be filled with dying uninsured people screaming in pain otherwise. The fact is, however, that anyone who goes anyplace other than a free clinic is going to be billed. Medicaid normally pays this bill for poor people. Private health insurance pays most of this bill for those who have it. There is a group in the middle, however, who by circumstances or by choice, roll the dice and lose.

I personally know someone who needed a simple appendectomy years ago. Uninsured and unable to pay, this person went to the emergency room. The procedure was done at a cost of $19,000. This person paid monthly payments for years in order to retire this debt and get on with her life.

Medical insurance is one of those things many young people either don't think about at all, or decide they don't need. They are, after all, young and invincible. The central tenet of the ACA is that a lot of young healthy people will subsidize older sick people. This "risk pooling" is how insurance works. Ironically, those young people who resent having to pay more to subsidize healthcare for older people are in many cases having their car insurance subsidized by older (statistically safer) drivers! Younger people will not be forced into buying health insurance. They will have the option, under the ACA, to pay a nominal fine instead. This fine, however, is not a coerced insurance premium. They will still be uninsured and running the very real risk that some unforeseen accident or illness will wipe them out for life.

Nearly all good companies offer their employees insurances very few of us think about. Oftentimes, they will even pay 100% of the premiums. Chief among these are short-term and long-term disability insurance, and life insurance.

Disability is a type of insurance that, while few people really think about it, we are far more likely to need at some point in our working lives than life insurance. Short-term disability covers you when you are unable to work for health reasons for a limited period of time. In the event you will be out of work longer, long-term disability kicks-in. Remember, you are three times more likely to become disabled than to die.

Life insurance is paid to your beneficiaries in the event of your death. Many companies offer a years' salary death benefit for free, no questions asked. Most offer up to five years' salary, although you may have to pay a portion of the premium and answer some questions about your health. Always answer health questions honestly. If you say you're a non-smoker but really smoke two packs a day, the insurance company will not pay the death benefit. Although not everyone needs life insurance (such as single young people with no dependents), always take whatever free insurance you are offered. You can always name me as your beneficiary!

Rich people generally load-up on life insurance. Though you will never know it if you claim it, it is something you provide for your family. Harry Gross, the old time radio host and financial columnist in Philadelphia used to say: "The man who dies without life insurance doesn't just die, he absconds." What this means is that a person who dies without providing for his or her spouse and children doesn't just die, but rips his or her family off by doing so.

If it takes $250,000 to raise a child, you need at least this much per child (as well as enough money to make sure this child has a house to grow up in.) There are two types of life insurance: "whole life" and "term life." Term insurance is almost always the better deal. Term insurance works like this: after vetting your medical history and giving you a medical examination, the insurance company will set your premium for a term of 10, 20, 30, or even 40 years. As long as you pay your premiums, you will remain insured. If you die during the term, your heirs will be paid. If you don't die you may be able to extend your term for a higher premium, or let the policy expire.

Not everybody needs life insurance. Once your children have grown and moved away and you have substantial assets, you don't need life insurance. Younger people, as I said, often don't need life insurance. Those without dependents would in most cases be better off saving their money for the day when they *do* have to pay life insurance premiums.

There is one final type of insurance I *really* hope you feel compelled to buy one day (hopefully as a result of reading this book). "Excess liability" or "umbrella" insurance is a type of insurance smart people with plenty of assets buy to further protect themselves. Although homeowner's policies generally cover you up to $500,000, umbrella insurance provides up to millions more. If a houseguest gets injured on your property and sues you for a million dollars, you're covered. If, in a fit of anger, you write a letter to the editor about that no-good lying county commissioner and he sues you for slander, you're also covered.

Not only is umbrella insurance great for your peace of mind, it's dirt cheap. A million dollars' coverage costs about $300 a year. The more coverage you buy, the cheaper it gets. If you have any appreciable amounts in taxable accounts (retirement accounts being generally protected from lawsuits), umbrella insurance is an absolute must.

Chapter Nine Takeaways

- Insurance is vital to protect what you've earned.

- Having *adequate* coverage is just as important as having coverage in the first place.

- Find out what kind of insurances you need.

- Always choose the highest deductible you can afford.

- Drop collision and comprehensive after your car has been paid-off for a few years.

- Once you have achieved affluence, umbrella insurance is a must.

X

Charlatans and Rip-off Artists

You get an email. It's from the former Minister of Finance of Nigeria. He needs to move $25,000,000 out of the country in a hurry. If you let him wire it to your bank account, he will pay you $3,000,000 for your trouble. You strongly suspect he did not come by this money legitimately, but it's not every day you get the chance to make a few million dollars for basically nothing. Your common sense tells you to delete the email and forget about it. Why did this formerly high ranking Nigerian government official pick your email address out of all the email addresses in America? It makes no sense, you think, as your finger searches-out the delete key. But wait. That's a lot of money. Think of what you could do with $3,000,000. It's ridiculous, your inner-voice persists. Wouldn't your bank be just a little bit suspicious of a $25,000,000 direct deposit when your bi-weekly deposit is around $800? Might not the F.B.I. or Interpol get involved? Your finger (very wisely) deletes the email before you can stop it. An hour later, after thinking about it, you laugh and wonder who could fall for such a scam. The answer is enough people that the scam has been going on for years with no signs of going away.

It is called a 419 scam, the Nigerian Scam, or advance-fee fraud. It might actually be funny if people hadn't been murdered or their life savings wiped-out over it. That anyone could believe it for even a second seems preposterous, but otherwise intelligent people can be and have been so swept up in the tangled web the scammers weave from Internet cafes in Lagos that they have actually gone to Nigeria to collect the money they were promised via email. The lucky ones have been arrested and expelled from the country for entering on false pretenses. An unlucky few have been murdered. None has ever actually gotten a dime.

In the late 80s I stopped at a truck stop in Maryland one dusky summer evening. No sooner had I stepped down from my truck than the creepiest looking guy I'd ever seen appeared from behind a trailer.

"Driver! Driver! Listen to me," he said with utmost urgency. "Did you hear about that driver that hit the lottery?"

"No," I said warily. Something was just not right.

"Come on! Come on! This driver's just about giving this money away. Hurry! Hurry!"

Like an idiot and not thinking very fast on my feet, I followed.

He led me through a maze of tractor-trailers. Pretty sure I was about to be robbed, I prepared myself mentally to either run, or if absolutely necessary, fight. Why I continued following is still beyond me looking back, but for some reason I very foolishly did.

We walked to the back of a trailer. A guy with a long white beard and a cowboy hat stood with cards spread-out on a piece of cardboard perched on an apple crate. He fanned a fistful of hundred dollar bills in my direction. He stood at least 6'6". Three other very shady men were standing around the "table."

Immediately coming to my senses, I turned and walked away. The guy who was originally waiting for me when I parked my truck started to follow. He shouted that I was crazy not to come get some of this money, but the big man stopped him, simultaneously waving me away. There would be other, better victims.

I was so nervous that I forgot why I'd stopped there in the first place. I got back into my truck and drove away.

I later learned that it was a "three card monte" scam. Three card monte is like a shell game, but instead of finding out where the pea is hidden after the shells have been shuffled around, you are looking for a queen of hearts. Like the pea in the shell game, you will never find this "money card" because it's not there. It has been removed by sleight of hand by the time the mark (victim) points to where he thinks it is. The other men standing around, I learned, were the shills. These are people who pretend to be players, but in fact are in on the elaborate scam. Shills often "win" three card monte hands, but marks never, ever, ever win even a single hand.

A few years ago in Paris, my wife and I saw a three card monte game being set up on a street corner in Montmartre. We hung back and watched. A man, eager to play, approached. After a quick lesson from the dealer, he started to win hand after hand. A crowd started to gather. The man was, I explained to my wife, a shill. The "lesson" was to show the tourists just how easy and winnable this game really was. We left before the police got there, but they always *do* eventually get there. That's why three card monte is played on a piece of cardboard on a crate. For quick escapes.

We found ourselves in Montmartre again a few days later. Who should we see but the dealer setting up his crate. A crowd gathered as he dazzled them with fast hands. Somebody approached, money in hand, eager to play. The dealer gave him a quick lesson. It was the same guy he'd given a lesson to a few days before, and who had "won" big.

Albert, one of the young guys in the office, shrieks.

"I'm rich! I'm rich! I'm #$&@%*+ rich!"

"What's going on over there?" Bill shouts from another cube.

"I just won two million dollars in the Dutch lottery!"

I shake my head and try not to snicker out loud. I am older, wiser, and more jaded now.

"Did you actually *play* the Dutch lottery, Albert?" I ask.

"Screw you, Lamb. You're just jealous."

"I'm not trying to burst your bubble, but how could you have won if you didn't play?"

"Screw you, Lamb. I was going to give everyone in this office 10 grand, but now you're not getting anything."

"Fair enough, Albert," I said, stifling a laugh. I just don't want to see you disappointed. You'll get another email soon asking you to send a 'processing fee.' Just tell them to take any fees you owe out of your winnings and send you the rest. If they say they can't and that you need to send them money first, you know it's a scam. You not only won't get anything from the Dutch lottery, but your 'processing fee' money will be gone."

A few hours later Albert caught up with me in the warehouse.

"Sorry I yelled at you, Lamb. You were right. They wouldn't take the processing fee out of the winnings. I guess there were no winnings."

There is an old saying in the con artist community (if that's what it's called) that "you can't cheat an honest man." This is not to say that anybody, including the most intelligent person, is immune to being ripped-off, but that the people who are the easiest marks let greed override their reason (and often their ethics). Anyone who would help launder $25,000,000 in ill-gotten gain is not completely honest. Illegal gambling is just that, illegal. In the one-in-a-trillion chance the Dutch lottery accidentally made a mistake and declared someone who didn't even play the winner, it would be unethical, to say the least, to accept the money.

Always listen to your gut. If something doesn't seem right, it most certainly isn't. Even if logic fails you (as it did me when I followed the three card monte shill to what might have been my robbery or worse) your gut usually won't. Mine saved me at the last minute. Don't be afraid of missing out. Zero percent of the wealthy people in America got that way by hiding money for a former Nigerian finance minister, winning at three card monte, or winning a foreign lottery they didn't play. If anything seems too good to be true, it's a virtual guarantee that it is.

Chapter Ten Takeaways

- Though no one is 100% immune from being ripped-off, con artists know the best marks are those who are a little bit shady themselves.

- No one just gives money away for no reason.

- If your gut tells you something doesn't seem right, listen!

XI

Giving It All Away (OK, Just Some of It)

Most rich people give at least something to charity. Some do it to get a tax deduction. Some do it to assuage feelings of guilt. More than a few do it to indulge massive egos; instead of not letting the left hand know what the right hand is doing (which is the hallmark of Christian charity), they want their name on the hospital wing to honor their "humble" contribution. Many rich and non-rich people alike give to charity to be seen as charitable. Watch the news or read the local paper around the holiday season and you will see many human interest stories featuring the more fortunate serving meals to the less fortunate, the more cameras the better, thank you very much. Some wealthy people, particularly business owners, give to spotlight their "community involvement." What they're really doing is advertising, the money sometimes literally coming out of the advertising budget. Finally, some people, rich and non-rich alike, give because they care.

Some years ago an extremely wealthy woman started placing automatic defibrillators in public buildings around New York City. When the press found out who she was and why she was doing this, she said something to the effect that "you can only have so many $30,000 vases until the novelty wears-off." She was, in my opinion, giving for the exactly right reasons.

With the exception of a handful of true sociopaths, most well-off people struggle with a feeling of unwarranted guilt at some time or other. Though where we end-up on the socioeconomic ladder is almost purely a result of good or bad decisions made by us (or our parents or grandparents), many wonder if they've received an over-generous slice of a finite pie or if they are just the beneficiaries of unearned and undeserved luck. This frequently results in one of two reactions: a hardening of the heart until one views the world as "makers" versus "takers," or an overwhelming need to be seen as charitable. Unfortunately, this need to be seen as charitable often devolves into moral vanity as rich people try to be more charitable (and thus holier) than thou.

The woman in New York was not giving to be seen. The press sought *her* out as she quietly went about saving lives. She was not giving to counter feelings of guilt. She apparently had plenty of $30,000 vases; she just concluded one more wouldn't do much for her. There was no indication that she regretted the $30,000 vases she *already* had. The woman did what she did simply because she had a sense, now so rare in the world, that she was her brother's keeper.

I despise charity. First and foremost, I despise it because it's necessary. Secondly, I despise it because it's so often completely ineffective. Thieves abound in the world of charitable giving. Many times the bigger part of your charitable dollar goes to hiring telemarketers and to giving sweet bonuses to CEOs of dubious "non-profits," while the intended recipients get the crumbs. Lastly, I despise charity because it very often gives the impression that the beneficiaries of it are the natural inferiors of the givers.

My favorite charity is actually not a charity at all. Kiva (Kiva.org) is an organization that grants microloans worldwide. It works like this: you (the donor) choose a small business enterprise and make a loan. It might be a seamstress in El Salvador, a farmer in Africa, or an upholsterer in Chicago. You decide which enterprise will get your loan. The loans are typically very small, usually in the neighborhood of $500 to $1,000. Though it might seem fantastical to the American mind, oftentimes something as seemingly insignificant as a sewing machine can have a massive butterfly effect. A woman in an impoverished village, for instance, can use this sewing machine to make clothes. She sells these clothes, which enables her to send her children to school. (Education is neither free nor compulsory in many parts of the world.) These children grow up and go on to universities. They become doctors, engineers, and businesspeople. When this happens enough times, GDP for the entire country grows. Millions are lifted out of poverty. A middle class eventually forms. This middle class consumes. Much of that consumption is imported from the United States. The guy who works at a factory in Wichita keeps his job because there are new consumers for the company's products.

Repayment rates on Kiva microloans are an astounding 99.02%! Kiva does a magnificent job of due diligence; the recipients of Kiva loans are vetted and taught the economics of credit. For their part, the loan recipients are not only ambitious, but people with a deep sense of dignity. Repayment is a matter of personal honor to the vast majority.

One thing I like about Kiva (and hate about charity in general) is the dynamic between donor and donee. Recipients of Kiva loans are not poor sheep to be gently herded and condescended to; they are your business partners. The relationship is one of equality. You provide a loan and get paid interest for it; the borrower gets access to capital, which all businesses need.

Charities should exist with the ultimate goal of going out of business. *Really* alleviating poverty on a mass scale would mean a charity's work is done. Unfortunately, charity doesn't have a great track record of alleviating poverty. In fact, it often perpetuates it. What does end poverty is rising GDP. Microlending is a small but crucial step in this process. Nobody does microlending better than Kiva for the "charitable" dollar.

Although I far prefer charities that "teach a man to fish" rather than "give a man a fish," there are some worthy charities out there that actually fulfill the primary function of a charity: to help people who truly need the help. The American Red Cross does fantastic work for people caught-up in natural disasters or those who suffer house fires. Catholic Charities not only provides shelter for the homeless, but mental healthcare and substance abuse treatment which are two huge contributors to homelessness in the first place. Many worthy causes can be found close to home. It's easy to ignore your local fire department or ambulance squad until you need them. Sometimes the best charity is given to a friend or relative in need. In this case you will not get a tax deduction. Also, it's better to *give* than to *lend* when helping family or friends because money can destroy relationships like few other things in this universe.

It's critical that you don't give money to bad charities. This just enables them to perpetuate themselves and keep the whole racket going. How do you know?

Charity Navigator is the definitive guide to charities good, bad, and fraudulent. It rates charities on a "star" system, four starts being exceptional, three stars being good, two "needs improvement," etc. It also provides alerts about really awful "charities" on its website. To look for a specific charity, just type the name in their search engine.

Just because you may not support a cause doesn't mean a charity for that cause is necessarily bad. There is, for instance, a highly rated charity for poets that gets four stars on Charity Navigator! While I have nothing against poets, this is not a charity I could support. I have always been of the mind that poets are supposed to struggle and make their fame and fortune posthumously. As the playwright George Bernard Shaw said: "There's no money in poetry, but then again, there's no poetry in money either!"

Chapter Eleven Takeaways

- Check-out any charities you are contemplating supporting on Charity Navigator.

- Don't give to businesses masquerading as charities.

- Ask yourself if the charity you're supporting is really helping or hurting.

XII

You: The Best Investment You Can Make

Sometimes just showing up is half the battle. Literally. I have seen numerous people fired for bad attendance over the years. Conversely, I have known people who would have been fired for serious mistakes made on the job but were saved by their reliability. Reliability is one of those intangible edges that is very easy to give yourself, but that an astounding number of people don't. Getting to work on time (or at all) each day, not leaving early, and doing the job at least adequately is seemingly a lot to ask of some people. That's a pity, because reliability often trumps intelligence, speed, and/or creativity. In a world where bosses answer to higher level bosses, a reliable employee is often the reason the middle manager comes out smelling like a rose. All but the most inept, terrible, and sociopathic bosses understand this. The smart ones do not take it for granted. They remember the reliable employee at evaluation time or when it comes time to give a merit raise, because they understand fully that reliability is one of those things most noticeable when it's not there. The higher level boss doesn't want to hear from the middle manager that the job didn't get done because no one would stay late to do it.

For the employee who chooses to pick the very low hanging fruit of reliability, the rewards can be immense. Reliability is intimately intertwined with reputation. A reputation, to paraphrase Warren Buffett, takes 20 years to build but only 20 seconds to destroy. A good reputation is virtually priceless. Sometimes the benefits of a good reputation fall out of the clear blue sky like manna from heaven, completely unexpected, even if you seem to be wasting your reliability on an unappreciative boss.

With the full disclosure that I have never been the fastest, smartest, or most creative person at any of my jobs, I have always striven to be the most reliable. The reason for this is that I am a devout believer in karma. Even if the boss was an ungrateful jerk, I have always believed that what comes around goes around eventually.

Little did I know what a weird trajectory fate would take that night "Valerie," a customer service representative at the company I was working for at the time, asked me to stay late to pull down pallets full of file boxes while she looked for the proverbial needle in the haystack.

I didn't particularly want to stay late this night. I didn't especially need the overtime. It was one of those early summer nights I enjoyed walking my dog, the type of night you recall wistfully in bleak December when it's already dark by quitting time. Still, I couldn't say no. Valerie was the very rare kind of customer service rep who remembered us warehousemen at Christmastime. She would swing by the warehouse on Christmas Eve with a card, an instant lottery ticket, and a small box of candy for each of the men. Karma demanded that I stay and help her without copping an attitude. I complied with karma's demands.

Words cannot sufficiently capture how boring it was to pull pallet after pallet out of the racks with a forklift, unwrap each one and hand Valerie each individual file box, re-wrap each one again when she didn't find the document she was looking for, put the pallet away, then repeat *ad nauseam*. Hours passed. I was getting hungry, but I wasn't going to take it out on her. Finally, at about 9:00 p.m., she found what she was looking for. She thanked me and I went home.

Four months later, "Barbara," another one of the customer service reps, hired my wife to play the harp at her wedding. She also invited me to the wedding as part of the deal. Most of the office people were there, but I didn't mind. Karma compels me to have a good rapport with everyone I meet.

I certainly wasn't thinking about networking *per se* as I made the rounds. I was having a great time. The food was excellent, the drinks free.

"Tom, I'd like you to meet my husband," Valerie said, introducing me. He was a nice guy. I'd heard he owned a company, but we didn't really talk business. We mostly talked about the Philadelphia Eagles.

I continued partying, mingling, and boasting (as modestly as I could) about some of the countries I had been to.

Later that night, as the reception was winding-down, Valerie's husband "Kevin" caught up with me again.

"We should go out for a beer sometime, he said, handing me his business card. "Let me get your number."

I got back into my usual routing the following Monday. I hadn't done or said anything embarrassing at the wedding, so everything was good.

A couple weeks later I noticed I had a message on my answering machine when I went home for lunch (as I did almost every day).

"Tom, this is Kevin -------. Please give me a call. I'd like to discuss an opportunity my company might have for you."

To make a long story short, Kevin offered me a job at an enormous salary. Though extremely grateful, I turned it down. I had gotten the opportunity to go to Antarctica by ship in the meantime. Wanderlust has always been my Achilles Heel. Although I have no regrets about reaching the bottom of the world, turning down that job is the one decision I've made in life that I've second-guessed the most.

It still amazes me that something as seemingly unremarkable as helping a coworker with an easy but tedious job on a single night would have *tripled* my salary had I taken the job.

For better or for worse, we are all commodities now. Where in the old days we were members of the company "family," now we are really just factors of production. As heartless as this new reality is, it does provide a certain freedom. Now, instead of being part of an enterprise, we *are* the enterprise. Our job is often just the revenue stream that funds this grand enterprise that is our life. If our labor is the commodity we sell, the objective should be to maximize the value of that commodity.

The obvious (and easiest) way to do this is to get an edge in the job you are already working. This can be as simple as showing up on time every day (which I already said, but which bears repeating) to projecting a good attitude at all times. This is easier said than done, especially if you feel taken for granted as so many of us do in an economy where companies currently have the upper hand and know it, but such seemingly small things do not go unnoticed. *Your* boss may pretend not to notice, but others in the company undoubtedly will.

Oftentimes, people in a specific industry will move from one company to another. Managers especially. I have personally seen cases where a boss will leave one company for a higher position at another. The first thing he or she then does (which companies hate) is to poach the best employees from the old place. This *always* results in the employee either getting a sweeter deal from the new company, or the old company offering them incentives to stay.

Because managers are well-connected, it's critical to understand that silence is golden. If you have nothing nice to say about your company or boss, say nothing at all. I once worked with a guy who interviewed with a competitor. He proceeded to tell the interviewer that so-and-so was sleeping with so-and-so, this other person was a crook, and that the whole company was probably shady. Not only did he not get the job he was applying for, he was immediately fired from the one he had when the interviewer promptly called a contact at the company right after the interview.

Demeanor is a very important intangible that can sometimes be a balancing act. No one likes a loudmouth or a sulker. You need to be a serious person in order to be taken seriously. Don't be the class clown. Many bosses will treat who they perceive to be immature as the children they imagine them to be. Also don't be humorless. No one likes to be around a brooding scowler they worry might go off at any moment. A chronic griper with a bad attitude does him- or herself no favors. I have yet to see or hear of a boss who realized the error of his ways because a complainer suddenly enlightened him after years of bitching about everything.

Although one ironclad law of economics is that of comparative advantage (essentially meaning that each person should concentrate specifically on his or her own job), bosses hate to hear "that's not my job" when asking an employee to do something else. While few bosses would have the nerve to ask a skilled machinist or an IT person to clean the bathrooms, it is not uncommon for supervisors to require employees to be "cross-trained." This should be seen as opportunity by the employee. The more jobs one can do, the more indispensable one becomes.

Despite the fact that apprenticeships are few and far between in the United States (unlike in Germany where trades are often taught on the job), sometimes companies will offer training that, when coupled with experience, can be pure gold to the employee. A warehouse worker who gets forklift certified gets a portable skill. A warehouse worker with proficiency in SAP (a computerized inventory system) can command top dollar. Even at the height of the Great Recession, those with shipping and receiving experience and a knowledge of international logistics could afford to be picky about which jobs they'd take. While education is directly correlated with income, not all education needs to come from an institution of higher learning. Sometimes the most lucrative opportunities come disguised as a nagging boss!

Speaking of education, it is a simple law of economics that college graduates will, with few exceptions, make more than high school graduates. A lot more. Wealthy people apparently understand the importance of education far better than some middle- and working class parents (who seem to have largely forgotten that one's child doing better than his parents is the aim and ultimate measure of success in America). It is for this reason that wealthy parents involve themselves heavily in their children's educations from an early age.

One criticism I often hear Americans make when trying to explain-away the fact that Chinese kids are so much "smarter" than American kids is that Chinese kids don't get a childhood. They go to school, then to piano lessons, then to tutoring, then to English lessons, then to bed. I might agree with this argument if so many American parents weren't just letting their children's childhoods pass in a haze of violent video games, barely literate texts full of inanities to friends, and no direction whatsoever.

Formal higher education should be approached carefully and thoughtfully. It is expensive, requires aptitude, and more work than many people expect or are willing to do. One horrible mistake many people make is to start and not finish. They leave the university with no degree and huge student loan debts. Universities, being businesses (as evidenced by their willingness to accept revenue-generating athletes who read at an elementary school level), will frequently accept students who are not ready. Many students get to college only to find themselves in need of remedial courses they should have taken in high school. With free online courses in almost everything, there is simply no good reason to pay big money for remedial courses. Anyone with the dedication to work through a free online intermediate algebra or English composition course not only proves that he or she has what it takes to succeed academically in college, but saves money on meaningless credits in the process.

Is one ever too old to go back to school? My answer to this question is: it depends. It makes no sense at all for a 50 year-old to take on large student loan debts with the idea that he or she will make it up with a well-paying new career. There simply isn't enough time left in most working lives to make the investment worthwhile. Some people, however, can benefit greatly by taking specific courses.

For some people, getting a college degree is not about money but about the accomplishment. This is a worthy goal. Education is one of those intangibles that, in the end, is usually worth far more to the person who achieves it than that sports car they bought 35 years ago. If the money it costs to obtain a degree will not have an adverse effect on the retirement of the person who seeks it, it's money well-spent indeed. (I can say with pride that the world's oldest college graduate is a fellow Tiger. Nola Ochs earned her degree from Fort Hays State University at age 95!)

One mistake many prospective students (and/or their parents) make is to look at the "hot careers of the future" articles in magazines and make academic decisions based solely on hoped-for future earnings. This is a mistake for several reasons. Not everybody is a STEM (science, technology, engineering, math) person. You are highly unlikely to be good at something you don't even like. Going to a job you hate every day for 40+ years makes for a long (and not particularly happy) life. Though many people have to work jobs they despise, it shouldn't be because they picked the wrong major.

There is a tidal wave of ignorance out there about certain majors. Liberal arts degrees are, according to the conventional "wisdom," useless. This is absolute hogwash. Liberal arts degrees are, in fact, very valuable. The most sought-after skill by industry today is the ability to communicate. Read any Internet message board to understand why. Those who can communicate in a foreign language, particularly a critical language such as Mandarin, Japanese, or Arabic, are at an extreme advantage. In a globalized business world a competent Mandarin speaker is at least as valuable to a company as an engineer, if not more so.

Should you decide to go back to school, *where* you go is far less important than *that* you go. Princeton may come with a lot of potential connections, but the accounting they teach there is the same accounting they teach at a state university. Studies have proven that people who go to public universities (which are usually far cheaper than private schools) make as much money over a career as people who go to private universities. For the adult working person planning to go back to school, my advice is to find a school that is cheap and *regionally* accredited. Regional accreditation is a must. This proves that the school is a real school and not a diploma mill. Some "for profit" universities claim to be "nationally" accredited, but national accreditation is utterly meaningless. If a school is not regionally accredited, it's not worth your time or money. Period.

Community college is a great place to start. For those snobs who look down their noses at community colleges, I would point out that, while easy to get in, once there the courses are as rigorous as most anywhere else. Credits earned at a community college are almost always transferrable to four year colleges. Anyone seeking a bachelor's degree would be wise to consider going to a community college for the first two years, because it can cut the cost of an education nearly in half!

I am a huge fan of online learning. Though its detractors have a lot to say, I have always believed that a good teacher can only really teach you how to teach yourself. Abraham Lincoln got his education almost entirely by reading books. So it is with online learning.

Online courses are *much* harder than courses taught in a classroom. It takes iron discipline to keep up, meet deadlines without a professor breathing down your neck, and to excel. Degrees earned entirely online are gaining wide-acceptance. Soon, the person who interviews you will just as likely be an online graduate. We are in the midst of a revolution in education made possible by technology and inevitable by a failure of colleges to contain costs.

A lot of well-regarded universities such as NYU, Drexel, and Penn State now offer degrees online. Should you decide to go this very tough route, it's crucial that you make sure the *online degree program* as well as the brick and mortar campus of the university is regionally accredited. It's possible (though I haven't heard of any cases) where an accredited university could offer an online degree that is not regionally accredited.

For those haters who claim that it's too easy to cheat with online education, allow me to introduce the CLA+. The "Collegiate Learning Assessment" is a standardized test, quickly growing in popularity, that proves that the person passing the test has a college-level grasp of academic topics. Though the CLA+ is criticized as too general by some, I think certifications of proficiency are the wave of the future. With free "open source" university lectures available online from some very prestigious universities, I think certifications in specific skills will be, if not the college degree of the future, at least the credential that gets many people the job.

Speaking of the job, there is now a free buffet of offerings that can help you in your present job or get you a new job if you are not inclined to pursue a college degree. In addition to the open source classes I wrote about in the preceding paragraph, the Internet provides a smorgasbord of great, free, valuable stuff amidst the cesspools of smut, scams, viruses, and malware. It is possible to take foreign language lessons for free. Fluent Spanish can earn the typical customer service representative a serious premium. All manner of accounting and business software tutorials can be found on the Internet. This won't get you a CPA, but could be the thing that gets you a well-paying office job. If you are proficient in Microsoft Office, no one needs to know that you got that way by watching Youtube videos!

When I was in high school, there was a definite bias against the kids who went to tech school. They were largely viewed by teachers and other students as pot-smoking slackers who just wanted to get out of going to "real" classes. Look who's laughing now.

That long ago arrogance has now resulted in a dire shortage of skilled tradespeople. A lot of parents back in those days thought their little Johnny was just too good to turn a wrench; now those kids who got their hands dirty four hours a day five days a week are making big money and have more job security than a radiologist. This trend will only accelerate as the old-timers continue to retire with no one to replace them. Where it is possible to transmit an X ray to be read by a foreign radiologist, you cannot outsource a burst water pipe.

If your kid shows an inclination for the skilled trades, encourage it! Not only can a plumber easily eclipse a doctor in net worth, but the education actually pays the student instead of the student starting his or her career with a pile of debt! Union apprenticeships usually last for five years and consist of a combination of classroom and (paid) hands-on work. Elevator repair is the most in-demand job in America. Along with air traffic controller, it is the one trade in which it is not at all uncommon to make six figures a year with just a high school diploma!

For the working adult who is not inclined to go to college and regrets never learning a trade, there is some good news. Many vocational-technical schools now offer adult evening programs at a nominal cost. Some community colleges have combined programs where you can learn a trade and earn a degree at the same time.

One area in which a wide gulf exists between the rich and the poor is in their health. The old-timers at my first real job out of high school, men loaded with aches and pains whose lives revolved around doctor's appointments, used to tell me that my health was my "first million bucks." The older I get, the more I can understand what they were talking about.

Working class people have far higher rates of smoking than either middle class or wealthy people. Poorer people also eat much more fat and sodium, and drink more soda. Sadly, it is much more expensive to eat well in the short run. Potato chips are cheaper than healthier snacks. Where wealthy people buy gym memberships, working class people are more inclined to watch TV after a hard day's work. Rich people are also much more likely to visit the doctor regularly.

I will not moralize here. (If I was a saint I would have told you by now.) Just let me say that quitting smoking not only rapidly improves your health no matter how long or heavily you've smoked, but is the single healthiest thing you can do for your bottom line. Although eating healthy generally costs more, some great healthy food can be had for dirt cheap at farmer's markets. If you drink, do so in moderation. Get out there and take a walk. It's cheaper than the gym, just as healthy, and affords you the opportunity to think about your investments.

See the doctor. If you're embarrassed because it's been way too long since your last checkup, he or she won't interrogate you about it. Most family doctors choose family medicine because they are understanding people. Think of a checkup as just another way of taking stock of yourself.

Thomas K Lamb

Take care of your health with at least the same commitment that you take care of your wealth. As Kerry Livgren of the great rock band Kansas wote: "All your money won't another minute buy."

Chapter Twelve Takeaways

- Intangibles such as reliability, punctuality, and a good attitude can go a long way towards making you indispensable.

- Experience coupled with on-the-job training can be pure gold!

- Education does not have to be formal.

- If you decide to pursue a degree, *cheap* and *regionally* accredited should be the watchwords for working adults.

- Don't overlook the skilled trades. The law of supply and demand bodes well for them for as far as the eye can see.

- Your health is your first million bucks.

Conclusion

Rich people are not rich because poor people are poor. Wealth is not a zero-sum game. No one needs to lose in order for you to win. Although the rich do enjoy some unfair advantages, there are other advantages they take that are available to everyone. As the narrative about income and wealth inequality heats-up, it's important for the working person to understand that he or she is not at the complete mercy of events. Decisions you make today will decide the outcome of tomorrow.

It doesn't matter who wins the next presidential election. Despite the campaign ads you will be inundated with, no mere President of the United States has the power over your life that you do. Those guys fawning over the congressman in the campaign commercials are actors. A factory worker doesn't enjoy a good life because some congressman makes it happen; he or she has to make that happen.

Financial success is an incremental process that requires a steady hand and a little knowledge, but not awful much else. There are no secrets to wealth. It takes no special genius to prosper far beyond what you might not have even considered to be within the realm of possibility.

Education, both the formal and the informal variety, is critical to your success. The ability to do due diligence can make you a fortune or at least prevent you from stumbling into disaster. Education, far more than a strong back, is the thing that can advance your career or give you a new and better one.

Most importantly of all, your health is your first million bucks.

Resources

Mutual Funds

Vanguard - www.vanguard.com

T.Rowe Price - www.troweprice.com

Fidelity - www.fidelity.com

Charles Schwab - www.schwab.com

Online Brokers

E*Trade - www.etrade.com

Scottrade www.scottrade.com

TD Ameritrade - www.tdameritrade.com

Sharebuilder - www.sharebuilder.com

Further Reading

Ordinary People, Extraordinary Wealth by Ric Edelman

The Intelligent Investor (Revised Edition) by Benjamin Graham

Thomas K Lamb

The Snowball: Warren Buffett and the Business of Life by Alice Schroeder

Warren Buffett Invests Like A Girl (And Why you Should, Too) by Louann Lofton

www.ingramcontent.com/pod-product-compliance
Lightning Source LLC
Chambersburg PA
CBHW051707170526
45167CB00002B/564